THE INFINITE HORIZON

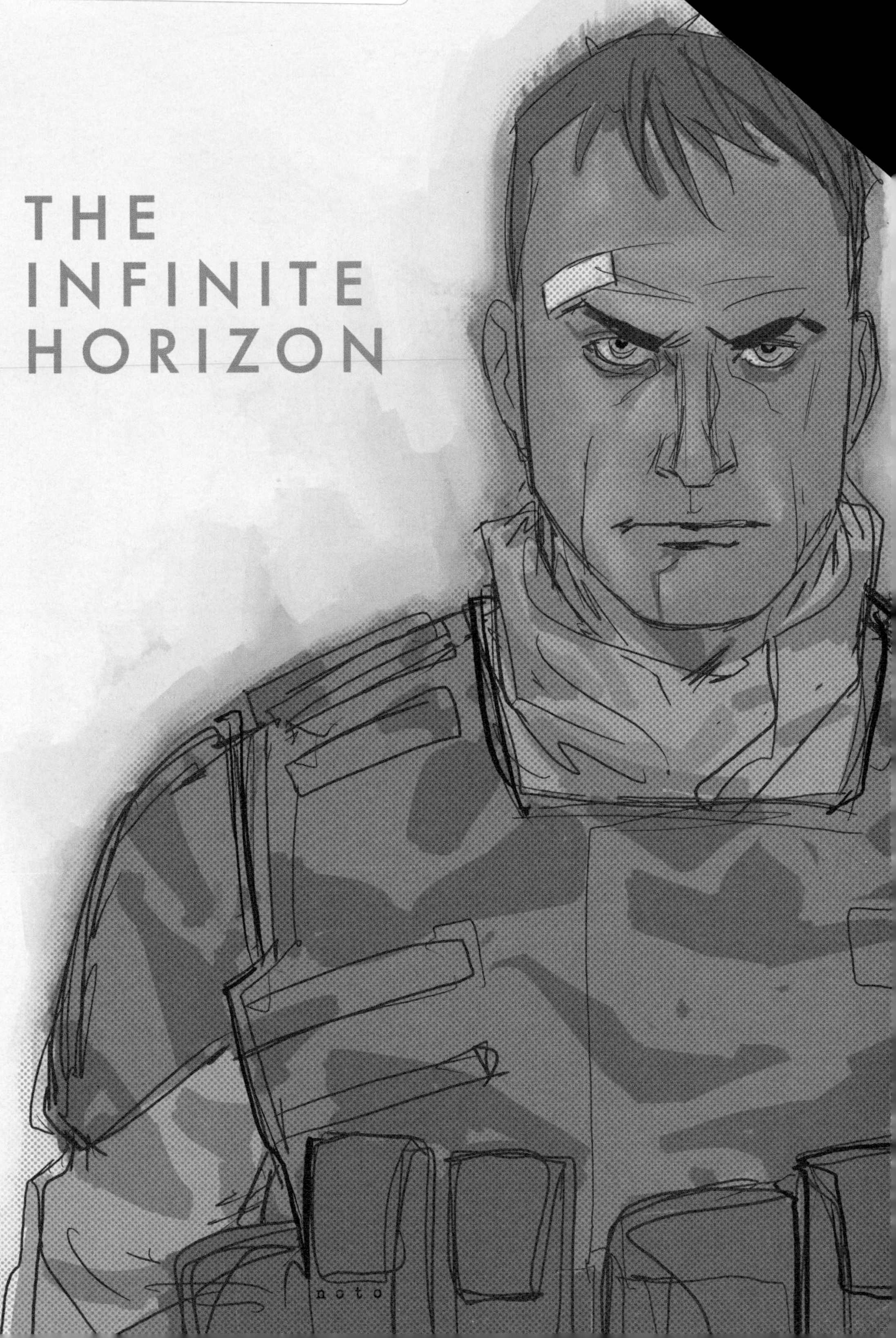

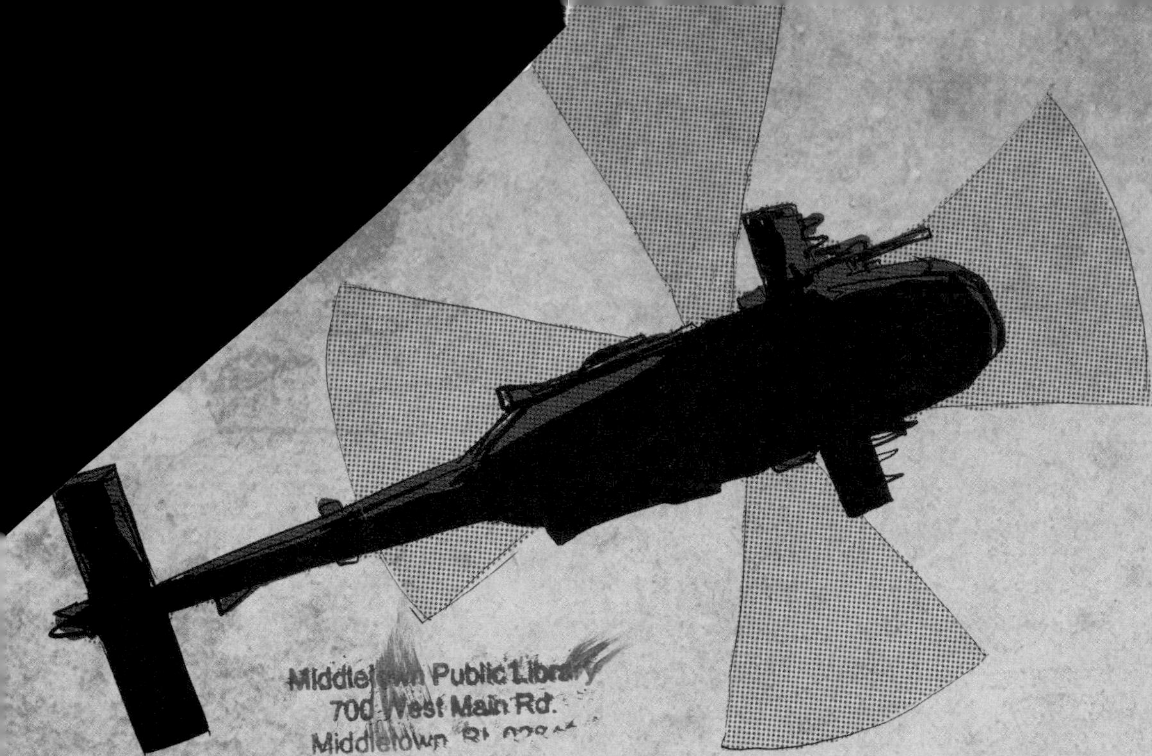

WRITTEN BY **GERRY DUGGAN**

ART BY **PHIL NOTO**

LETTERING BY **ED DUKESHIRE**

BOOK DESIGN BY **DREW GILL**

THE INFINITE HORIZON. Second printing. October 2012. ISBN: 978-1-58240-972-6

IMAGE COMICS INC.
www.imagecomics.com

This is a story that takes a circuitous route, so bear with me. It begins in the 1970s, with my parents buying me comic books. My father commuted from our home in Ridgewood, New Jersey to Manhattan five days a week, and the forty minute train ride demanded reading material. He would buy a paper for himself and, if I was lucky, he would show up at home with a *Spider-Man*, *Hulk*, or *Batman* comic. My mother might buy me something to read from a grocery store check-out line.

Comic books became my first love.

Skipping over the '80s is a good idea when possible, so let's jump to the evening the first Gulf War began, in 1991. America watched a war begin on TV. I recall thinking the surreal experience was right out of *The Dark Knight Returns*, but I digress. We were at war, and my father told me I might be heading up to Canada if there was a draft. It was a joke, but not a joke.

My dad grew up in the Catskill Mountains of upstate New York. His first plane trip was to Vietnam. He spent the summer of 1969 fighting in the jungles of Southeast Asia while America landed on the moon, and the rest of the world literally gathered in his backyard for Woodstock. He returned home with a bronze star, purple heart, and a loathing of war.

Of course, my fear of being flung across the world to foreign sands lasted for just one night, but fear only needs a few moments to do its work. Before long, a war I did not want—or even understand—was over, but the idea of being shipped halfway across the globe to fight stayed with me. I graduated high school, college and eventually settled in Los Angeles, and began writing anything I could for money.

Rick Remender introduced me and Brian Posehn to Image Comics, and the result was a *The Last Christmas*, the true story of Santa Claus after the apocalypse. It was my first taste of making something that was free from interference. Creator-owned comics is pure. I got addicted.

The end of the world is always fun to think about, and around this time America went back into Iraq. Things happen faster now: I met my future wife, Virginia. I re-read her copy of *The Odyssey* after she moved in. David Mandel introduced me to the obscenely talented Phil Noto. He shares my love of apocalypse stories, westerns and comics. The seeds for this comic were all growing nicely.

By this time, I'm making a living writing for television but I want to try something else. I asked Phil what he thought of re-imagining of *The Odyssey* in our near future. He told me he was all in, and helped shape the story. Erik Larsen said "yes" and we shake on it at a convention. Our first few issues sold well, and are reviewed even better. Joe Keatinge phones from Image. Suddenly we were Eisner nominees. It felt like this was happening to someone else.

Then everything slowed down. Phil and I each welcomed a son to the world. Life got in the way of the passion project. Our miniseries was late. Then later. And finally lost.

Now found.

We apologize for the delay, but we're thrilled to have completed the book you now hold in your hands.

The Infinite Horizon wouldn't be possible without Ed Dukeshire's contribution. His dynamic lettering and effects made our work pop off the page. Kudos, Ed. I hope we can do it all again soon. I would personally like to thank Phil. He can do anything he wants...and he did a comic with me. I'll always be grateful to him for making this dream come true.

We must thank the many talented, hard working people at Image that helped make this comic a reality. True professionals all. We would have been lost without them.

Special thanks to Eric Stephenson, Joe Keatinge, Jim Demonakos, Drew Gill, David Mandel, Kelvin Mao, Blair Butler, Ford Lytle Gilmore, Harris Miller, Rick Remender, Brian Posehn, Patton Oswalt and our families for the many evenings lost to *The Infinite Horizon*. We're grateful to the fans and retailers that bought the single issues, and of course we'd like to thank you for buying this book.

Finally, I don't want to toot our own horn, but it took Odysseus ten years to get home. We did it in half.

Best Regards,

Gerry Duggan
Home In Los Angeles, 2012

PRELUDE TO
THE INFINITE HORIZON

HERE I AM, MY LOVE, BACK IN A WORLD OF DEATH... SACRIFICING SO MUCH FOR SO LITTLE IN RETURN.
WHOOOM
SKREEEEEEEEEE
HOW THE HELL DID I GET BACK HERE?

I'D FOUGHT THEIR WARS WITH RIGHTEOUS ANGER BEGINNING WITH AFGHANISTAN...
...BUT MY FIRE HAD GONE OUT LONG BEFORE WE LANDED IN SYRIA.
MOVE. QUICKLY.
OUR COUNTRY HAD BECOME THE WORST KIND OF GAMBLER: DOUBLING ITS BETS TRYING TO END AN EXCRUCIATING LOSING STREAK.
MAYBE IT WAS INEVITABLE AFTER TEL AVIV.

< IT'S EMPTY! >
IT WASN'T COMPLETELY EMPTY.
DEET

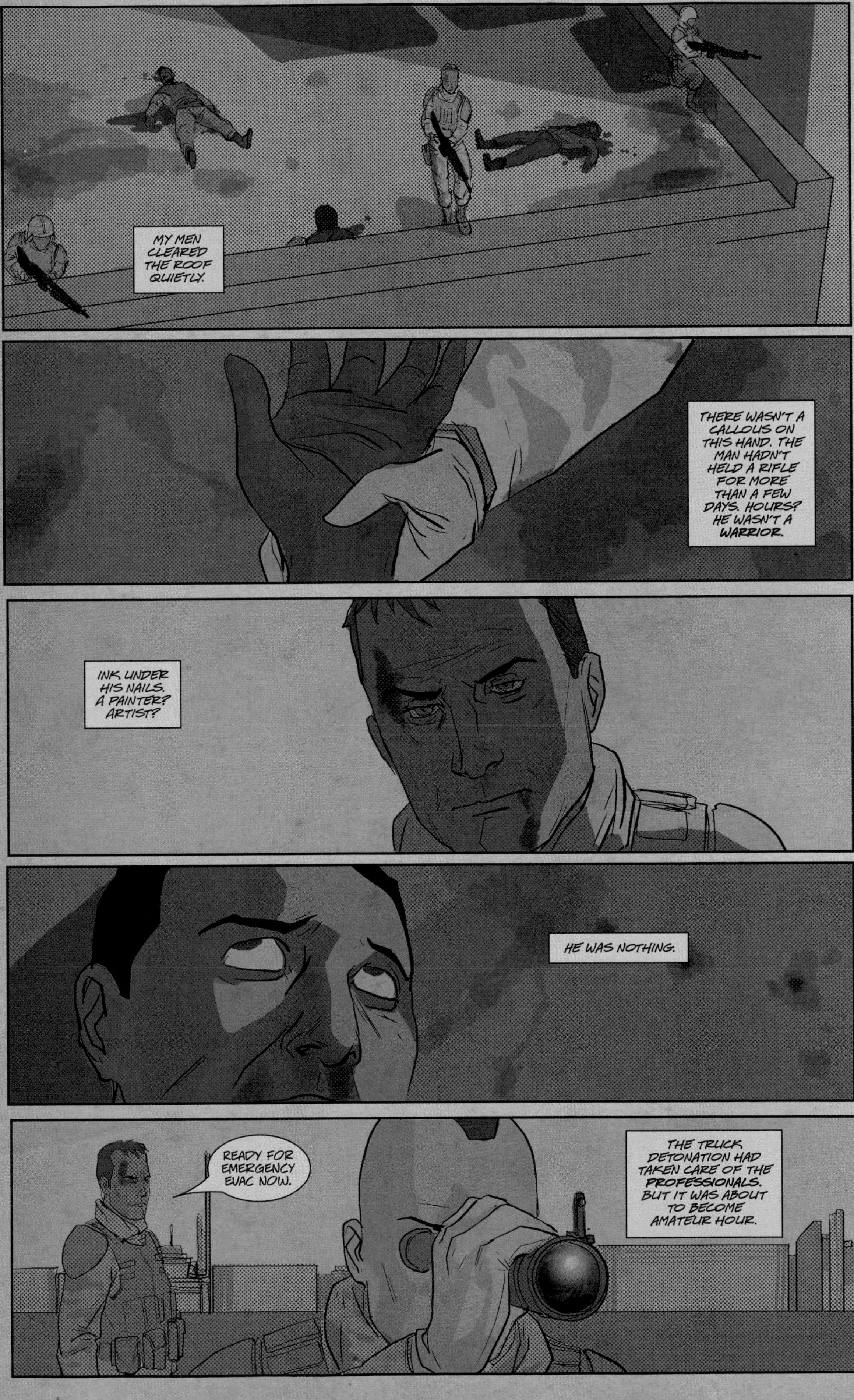
MY MEN CLEARED THE ROOF QUIETLY.
THERE WASN'T A CALLOUS ON THIS HAND. THE MAN HADN'T HELD A RIFLE FOR MORE THAN A FEW DAYS. HOURS? HE WASN'T A WARRIOR.
INK UNDER HIS NAILS. A PAINTER? ARTIST?
HE WAS NOTHING.
READY FOR EMERGENCY EVAC NOW.
THE TRUCK DETONATION HAD TAKEN CARE OF THE PROFESSIONALS. BUT IT WAS ABOUT TO BECOME AMATEUR HOUR.

IF I HAD ORDERED MY MEN TO ENGAGE-- WE WOULD HAVE BEEN VICTORIOUS.
8872-GK
CO-TRA : 654m
ODDS ARE I WILL WIN EVERY BATTLE I'M EVER IN. BUT NOT THE WAR. NOT THIS WAR. I'VE SEEN THAT FOR SOME TIME.
THE MEN UNDER MY COMMAND HAD COME TO THE SAME REALIZATION. IT WAS IN THEIR EYES.
WE ALL MISSED HOME. WE DIDN'T KNOW IT AT THE TIME... BUT HOME MIGHT AS WELL HAVE BEEN ON THE MOON.

THE MEN RUNNING THE SHOW NEVER VENTURED BEYOND THE WALLS AND NOTHING INSIDE OF THEM WAS REAL-- SO THEY NEVER SAW THE TRUTH.
BLOOD WOULD WASH THE ARROGANCE FROM THEIR FACES. WHEN IT HAPPENED -- IT WOULDN'T BE BECAUSE I DIDN'T DO MY JOB.
BUILDING NATIONS THE AMERICAN WAY
I SERVED PROUDLY...WITH HONOR AND DISTINCTION.
THAT MEANT NOTHING TO THE PIGS AT THE TROUGH.
GODDAMMIT! GET BACK HERE!

I KNOW YOU WILL COME BACK FOR ME. YOU MUST. BECAUSE IF YOU DON'T-- I WILL DIE...
...AND OUR SON ALONG WITH ME.
YOU HAVE BEEN GONE SO LONG THAT I HAVE ALMOST FORGOTTEN YOUR TOUCH...
AND THESE MEN HAVE FORGOTTEN YOUR FRIENDSHIP...
THEY'RE HERE TO ENSURE THE WATER THAT FLOWS THROUGH OUR LANDS CONTINUES TO IRRIGATE THEIRS.
BUT IF THEY CAN DOMINATE OUR HOUSE--THEY WILL CONTROL FRIEND AND ENEMY ALIKE FOR MILES AROUND. I HAVE MAINTAINED A FRAGILE TRUCE--BUT FOR HOW LONG?

HOW LONG CAN I SURVIVE WITHOUT YOU?
YOU'VE WAITED SO LONG ALREADY. JUST BE PATIENT A LITTLE WHILE LONGER.
SIR.
THEY HAD COME FOR ME. THEY DIDN'T HAVE A CHOICE. I DIDN'T GIVE THEM ONE.
I'M READY.
I'LL CRAWL THROUGH HELL TO RETURN TO YOU, PENELOPE.

WE HAVE BANDED TOGETHER. THERE'S **STRENGTH** IN NUMBERS. THE TIDES ARE RIGHT TO TRAVEL SAFELY AGAIN.
...AND WHEN YOU ARRIVE YOU'LL BE WELCOMED WITH OPEN ARMS BY A GROUP THAT HAS NOT JUST SURVIVED THE WORST...
HUFF HUFF
...BUT **THRIVED.**
OH GOD!
HUFF... GOD...
STAND BY FOR COORDINATES--

SAVE ME.
HOW ARE YOU TODAY, MY LOVE?
FUCKING DIE.
IF I GO, SO DO YOU.

GOOD. I HOPE WE BOTH DIE. I PRAY EVERY DAY FOR SOMEBODY TO KILL YOU.
WHO IS GOING TO KILL ME? YOU?
HEH.
WHO IS GOING TO FIND US HERE?
THIS IS THE *END* OF THE *EARTH*.
THE BEGINNING

CHAPTER ONE
"Journey Into Misery"

GETTING BACK HOME TO HER WAS MY GREATEST ACHIEVEMENT.
I WAS AWAY FOR YEARS... VOLUNTEERING FOR AFGHANISTAN, AND THEN SENT TO IRAQ, AND LATER...EVERYWHERE ELSE MY COUNTRY CHASED SHADOWS.
IN THE END, THE MEN CALLING THE SHOTS RAN TERRIFIED WHEN THEY REALIZED THEIR WAR EVOLVED INTO SOMETHING THAT COULDN'T BE WON WITH THE GUN. BECAUSE AMERICA DOESN'T KNOW ANY OTHER WAY TO FIGHT.
THE WAR THAT NEVER RAN SHORT OF BLOOD JUST...QUIETLY RAN OUT OF GAS. BUT I ACCOMPLISHED MY FIRST MISSION: I HAD SOMEHOW FUCKING LIVED.
AFTER THE YEARS WE SACRIFICED FOR THE WAR...NEITHER OF US DESERVED THE TORTURE THAT WAS TO COME.
AFTER I TOOK OFF THE UNIFORM...THE REAL HELL BEGAN.
YEARS MORE BURNT GETTING HOME...AND SHE WAITED FOR ME.

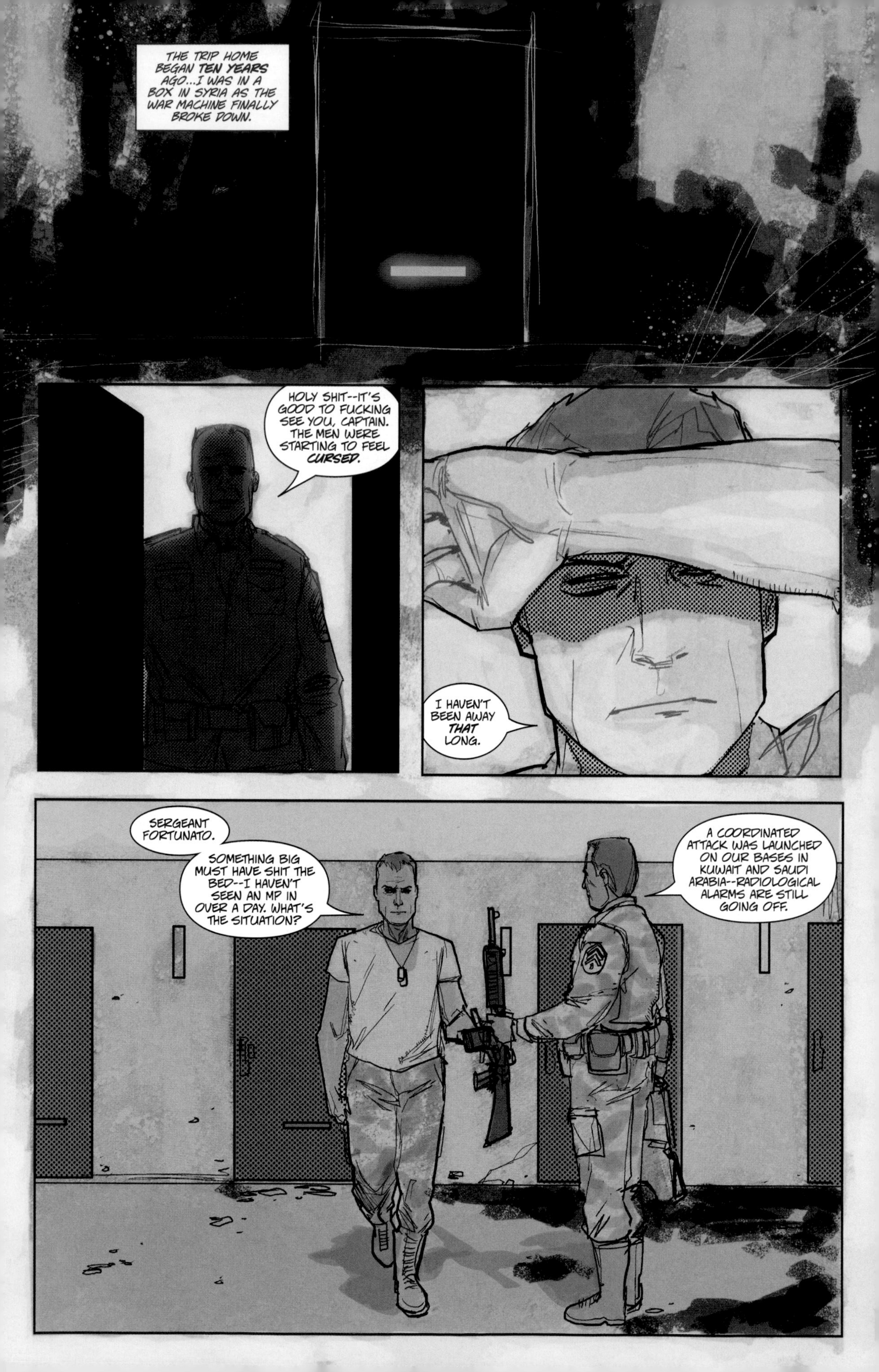
THE TRIP HOME BEGAN TEN YEARS AGO...I WAS IN A BOX IN SYRIA AS THE WAR MACHINE FINALLY BROKE DOWN.
HOLY SHIT--IT'S GOOD TO FUCKING SEE YOU, CAPTAIN. THE MEN WERE STARTING TO FEEL CURSED.
I HAVEN'T BEEN AWAY THAT LONG.
SERGEANT FORTUNATO.
SOMETHING BIG MUST HAVE SHIT THE BED--I HAVEN'T SEEN AN MP IN OVER A DAY. WHAT'S THE SITUATION?
A COORDINATED ATTACK WAS LAUNCHED ON OUR BASES IN KUWAIT AND SAUDI ARABIA--RADIOLOGICAL ALARMS ARE STILL GOING OFF.

AT THE SAME TIME THE MAJORITY OF THE SAUDI ROYAL FAMILY WERE ASSASSINATED DURING THE PRINCE'S WEDDING.
THE KINGDOM'S OIL FIELDS WERE HIT TOO--THERE'S NO OIL FLOWING ANYWHERE IN THE MID EAST.
BUT THAT'S NOT THE BIG NEWS.
CHINA FINALLY WENT INTO TAIWAN LAST NIGHT--THE FIRST THING THEY DID WAS KNOCK OUT OUR SATELLITES.
Uplink Failed.
Run Diagnostics?
THEY BLINDED MOST EVERYTHING UP THERE WITH EMP'S AND THEY NAILED THE HARDENED MILITARY SATELLITES IN LOW EARTH ORBIT THE OLD FASHIONED WAY: SHOT THEM DOWN.
ANY GOOD NEWS?
YEAH, WE'RE GOING HOME. THE COLONEL ORDERED ME TO BRING YOU TO THE AIRPORT.
SOME OF OUR PLANES ARE EVACUATING TO AFGHANISTAN BECAUSE THERE'S NOT ENOUGH FUEL TO GET TO GERMANY! WE'RE EVAC'ING BACK TO TALIBAN COUNTRY!

WE SIMPLY DON'T HAVE ENOUGH ASSETS TO GET EVERYONE OUT RIGHT AWAY. ADDITIONAL FLIGHTS ON CIVILIAN CARRIERS ARE BEING SET UP-- BUT THAT EQUIPMENT WON'T START ARRIVING UNTIL TOMORROW. HUNKER DOWN FOR NOW. THAT'S ALL.
CAPTAIN, A MOMENT?
I GOT A REAL KICK OUT OF YOU KNOCKING THOSE CONTRACTORS ON THEIR ASSES. HOPE THE DAYS YOU SPENT IN THE COOLER WERE WORTH IT.
HARD TO ARGUE WITH THE RESULTS, SIR.
I'M PUTTING YOU IN CHARGE OF SECURING AND HOLDING THIS AIRPORT UNTIL THE EVAC IS COMPLETE. I KNOW YOU'LL DO EVERYTHING YOU CAN.
YES, SIR.
THE NEXT FEW DAYS ARE GOING TO BE... CHAOTIC. CIVILIAN EMPLOYEES FROM ACROSS THE REGION NEED TO BE AIRLIFTED.
THIS IS THE LAST PACKET I DOWNLOADED BEFORE WE LOST ALL COMMUNICATIONS.
MARTIAL LAW WAS DECLARED BACK HOME. THE MEN ARE LIKELY TO BE DEPLOYED INTO THE STREETS WHEN THEY LAND. KEEP IT NEED-TO-KNOW UNTIL THEY'RE IN THE AIR.
LEVEL 5 CLASSIFIED
OPERATION THEMISTOCLES
Re: EVACUATION CONTINGENCIES

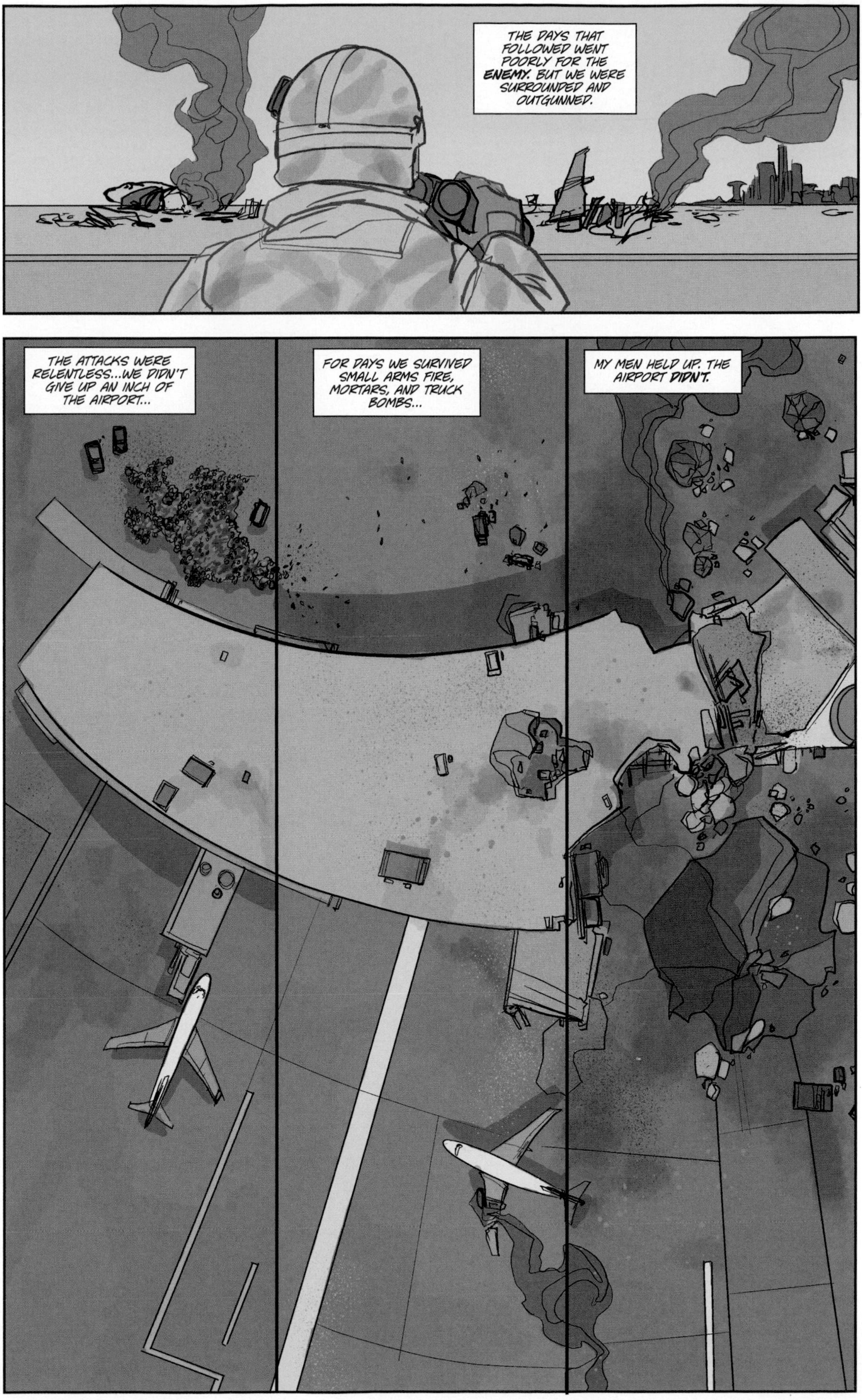
THE DAYS THAT FOLLOWED WENT POORLY FOR THE ENEMY. BUT WE WERE SURROUNDED AND OUTGUNNED.
THE ATTACKS WERE RELENTLESS...WE DIDN'T GIVE UP AN INCH OF THE AIRPORT...
FOR DAYS WE SURVIVED SMALL ARMS FIRE, MORTARS, AND TRUCK BOMBS...
MY MEN HELD UP. THE AIRPORT DIDN'T.

GO AHEAD, FAR SUPPORT.
FAR SUPPORT IS EXTRACTING. OUR CARRIER GROUP WILL BE OUT OF RANGE AFTER THIS RUN...GOOD LUCK, CAPTAIN. WE'RE HEADING HOME.
BOOM
SEE YOU BACK THERE.
HOME. MAYBE IF I FLEW JETS I COULD THINK ABOUT HOME ALL DAMN DAY.
CAP, YOU GOTTA SEE THIS.
DON'T THINK ABOUT HOME. SHE'S STILL HALF A WORLD AWAY.
NOT EVERYONE DOWN THERE IS GOING TO MAKE IT OUT BEFORE THE FLIGHTS STOP... WE'VE PASSED UP FLIGHTS ALL DAY. HOW LONG DO YOU INTEND TO STICK IT OUT?
YOU'RE RIGHT.
HOLD THE MEN BACK. KEEP BOARDING THE WOMEN AND CHILDREN. AND START LOADING THEM INTO THE CARGO COMPARTMENTS.
HOLY SHIT-- ARE YOU--ARE YOU SERIOUS? IS THAT SAFE?

NO.
IT ISN'T SAFE AT ALL.
PHWAM!
PHWAM!

GET DOWN THERE AND TELL OUR GUYS TO ASSEMBLE. THIS POSITION WON'T HOLD FOR LONG.
HALLELUJAH!
WE KNEW THIS WAS ONLY THE EYE OF THE HURRICANE. THE ENEMY RUSHED US AS SOON AS THEY REALIZED THE AIR SUPPORT FROM THE CARRIERS HAD FINALLY DRIED UP.
GOD DAMN IT.
I CURSED MYSELF FOR LETTING MY MIND WANDER BACK HOME.
BACK TO HER.

CATSKILL MOUNTAINS, NEW YORK
I KNOW YOU'RE ALL WORRIED ABOUT WHAT IS TO BECOME OF YOUR LAND. I WANT TO ASSURE YOU THAT WHAT WATER WE HAVE IS ALSO YOURS. WE WILL CONTINUE TO MAKE WATER RATIONS AVAILABLE TO ALL THE PROPERTIES WE CAN.
LAST MONTH'S... TROUBLES ARE OVER. I REGRET WHAT HAPPENED--BUT I THINK WE'VE SEEN WHAT FEAR AND GREED CAN DO TO US. I HOPE THAT PROBLEM IS BEHIND US NOW.
I'M SURE YOUR FAMILIES AND YOUR FARMS... OR CAMPS NEED YOU BACK HOME. PLEASE.
IF I MAY, PENELOPE--WE TRUST YOU--IT'S EACH OTHER WE DON'T TRUST.
AND WITH GOOD FUCKING REASON! WHAT HAPPENED HERE DIDN'T HAVE TO HAPPEN WITH A LITTLE MORE CONSIDERATION. THREE GOOD MEN ARE DEAD BECAUSE--

GOOD MEN?! YOU BASICALLY HELD EVERYONE TO THE EAST OF HERE HOSTAGE!
THE WATER BELONGS TO EVERYBODY-- NOT JUST THE PEOPLE WITH THE MOST LAND!
UFF
WE SAY IT OVER AND OVER!
GAH
STOP! STOP IT!
THEY'RE GREEDY, FEARFUL, AND DESPERATE. GOD HELP ME.
HE'LL KNOW WHAT TO DO WHEN HE GETS BACK.

IT'S HEAVY.
WON'T BE FOR LONG. NEXT SEASON IT WILL SEEM PERFECT--AND THE YEAR AFTER IT MIGHT BE TOO SMALL. REMEMBER--YOU WANT TO LEAD YOUR TARGET. A DEER MIGHT BE MOVING. YOU DON'T WANT TO AIM WHERE YOUR TARGET *IS*--YOU WANT TO BE ABLE TO HIT WHERE IT *WILL* BE.
TERRENCE! PUT THAT *DOWN!*
GET INSIDE THIS INSTANT! MR. HULL, YOU ARE *NEVER* TO PUT A *GUN* INTO MY SON'S HANDS!
WASN'T LOADED, PENELOPE. BESIDES, I'M JUST TRYING TO HELP TERRY WHILE HIS FATHER IS...GONE.
HIS FATHER WILL RETURN SOON-- AND *HE* WILL TEACH TERRENCE WHEN HE'S OLD ENOUGH.
DIDN'T MEAN NO DISRESPECT--
HEY, HULL-- WHY DON'T YOU GO HELP YOUR BUDDY-- HE'S GONE AND GOTTEN HIS *OTHER ARM* BROKEN.
YOU SONS OF BITCHES. DON'T YOU UNDERSTAND THAT THIS FIGHTING IS ONLY GOING TO HURT YOU?
IT'S GONNA COME AROUND ON YOU, BURKE. I *PROMISE*.

THANK YOU. YOU'VE ALWAYS BEEN A GOOD FRIEND TO MY HUSBAND. TO US.
THINK NOTHING OF IT. HOW LONG ARE YOU...GOING TO PUT UP WITH THIS?
EVERYONE'S JUST SCARED. AFRAID OF LOSING WELL WATER... AFTER LOSING SO MUCH ELSE. THIS FAMILY HAS NEVER PLAYED POLITICS WITH THE WATER HERE.
THE MEN HERE TRUST YOU--THAT WAS NEVER THE ISSUE. BUT, WITH THE EXODUS OF PEOPLE FROM DOWNSTATE AFTER EVERYTHING THAT HAPPENED IN NEW YORK--IT CAN BE HARD TO KNOW WHO'S A FRIEND--AND WHO ISN'T. PEOPLE ARE SCARED.
EVERYONE WILL FEEL BETTER WHEN MY HUSBAND RETURNS.
PENELOPE... WHAT IF HE *DON'T?*
GOOD NIGHT, MR. BURKE.
I'M SORRY--

I WISH YOU WOULD QUIT TRYING THAT EVERY FIVE MINUTES.
YOU PROMISED IT WOULD BE **FIXED** SOON.
I WAS **WRONG**.
*I HAVEN'T HEARD FROM YOU. BUT I KNOW THE **WAR IS OVER**. I KNOW YOU'RE ON YOUR WAY BACK TO ME. YOU HAVE TO BE.*
YOU BETTER BE. OR I'LL KILL YOU.

I WAS STILL IN A WAR ZONE BUT MY MIND WAS DRIFTING BACK HOME. DANGEROUS. EASY WAY TO DIE.
HOW THE HELL ARE WE GETTING OUT OF HERE?
THERE WAS NO EASY WAY OUT. WE HADN'T SEEN A PLANE LAND IN SEVERAL HOURS...
...WELL, NOT ON A RUNWAY ANYWAY.
CRACK OPEN THIS LUGGAGE--FIND CIVVIE CLOTHES FOR YOURSELVES. DUMP ANYTHING NONESSENTIAL FROM YOUR GEAR.

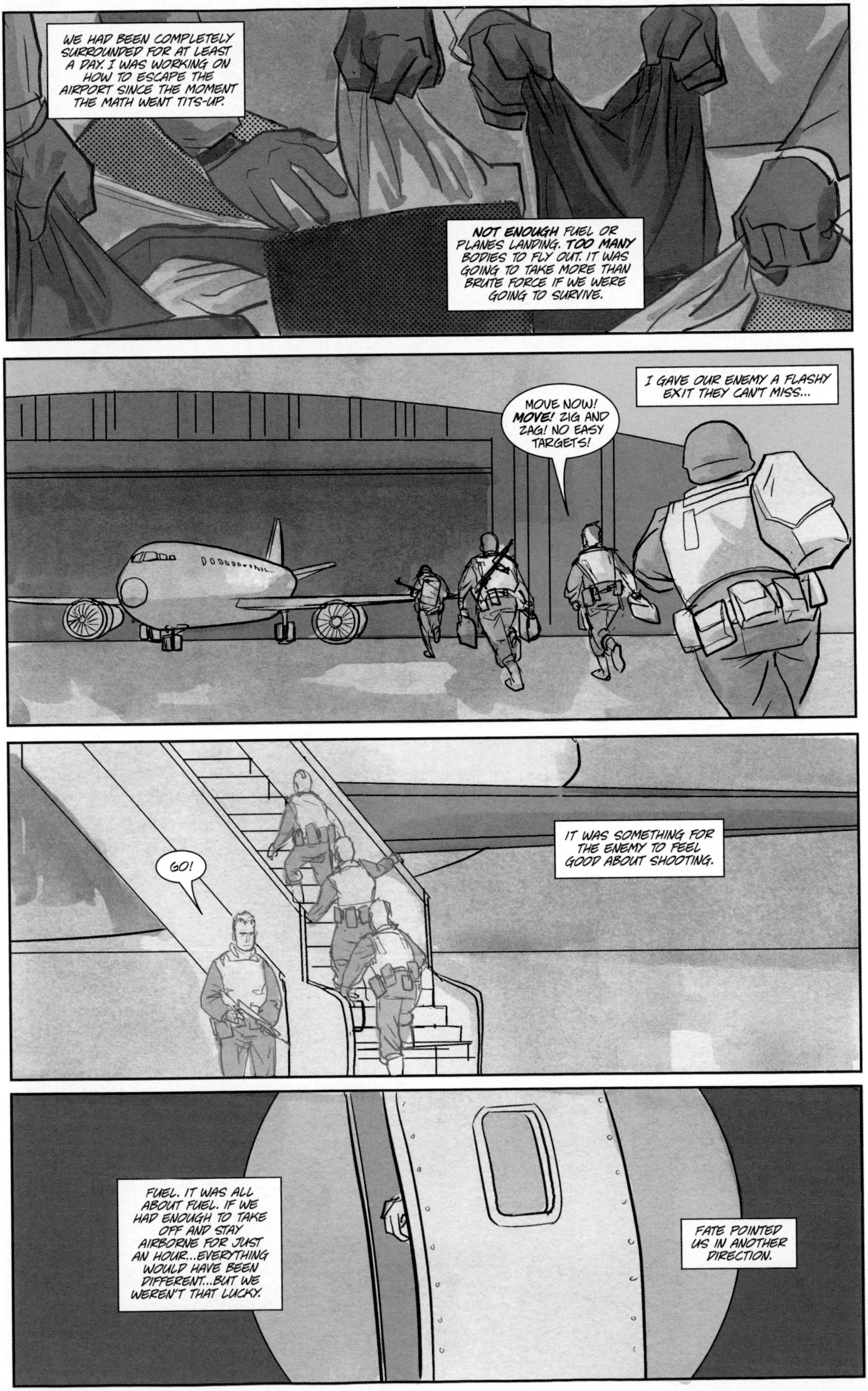
WE HAD BEEN COMPLETELY SURROUNDED FOR AT LEAST A DAY. I WAS WORKING ON HOW TO ESCAPE THE AIRPORT SINCE THE MOMENT THE MATH WENT TITS-UP.
NOT ENOUGH FUEL OR PLANES LANDING. TOO MANY BODIES TO FLY OUT. IT WAS GOING TO TAKE MORE THAN BRUTE FORCE IF WE WERE GOING TO SURVIVE.
I GAVE OUR ENEMY A FLASHY EXIT THEY CAN'T MISS...
MOVE NOW! MOVE! ZIG AND ZAG! NO EASY TARGETS!
IT WAS SOMETHING FOR THE ENEMY TO FEEL GOOD ABOUT SHOOTING.
GO!
FUEL. IT WAS ALL ABOUT FUEL. IF WE HAD ENOUGH TO TAKE OFF AND STAY AIRBORNE FOR JUST AN HOUR...EVERYTHING WOULD HAVE BEEN DIFFERENT...BUT WE WEREN'T THAT LUCKY.
FATE POINTED US IN ANOTHER DIRECTION.

THERE WAS BARELY ENOUGH FUEL TO KEEP THE ENGINE BLADES SPINNING--
--BUT THAT'S ALL THEY HAD TO DO. IF THE ENEMY THOUGHT WE WERE TRYING TO FLY OUT...
WE MIGHT BE ABLE TO SLIP AWAY.
KKKRAK
UNG-
SET THE CHARGES NOW, FORTUNATO!
ALMOST DONE...ONE SECOND MORE--
WE DON'T HAVE ANOTHER SECOND!
I WAS GOING TO GET US OUT OF SYRIA.

JUST NOT BY PLANE...AND NOT QUICKLY.
HIT THE GROUND RUNNING.
FIRE IN THE HOLE!
SKRAABOOOOM

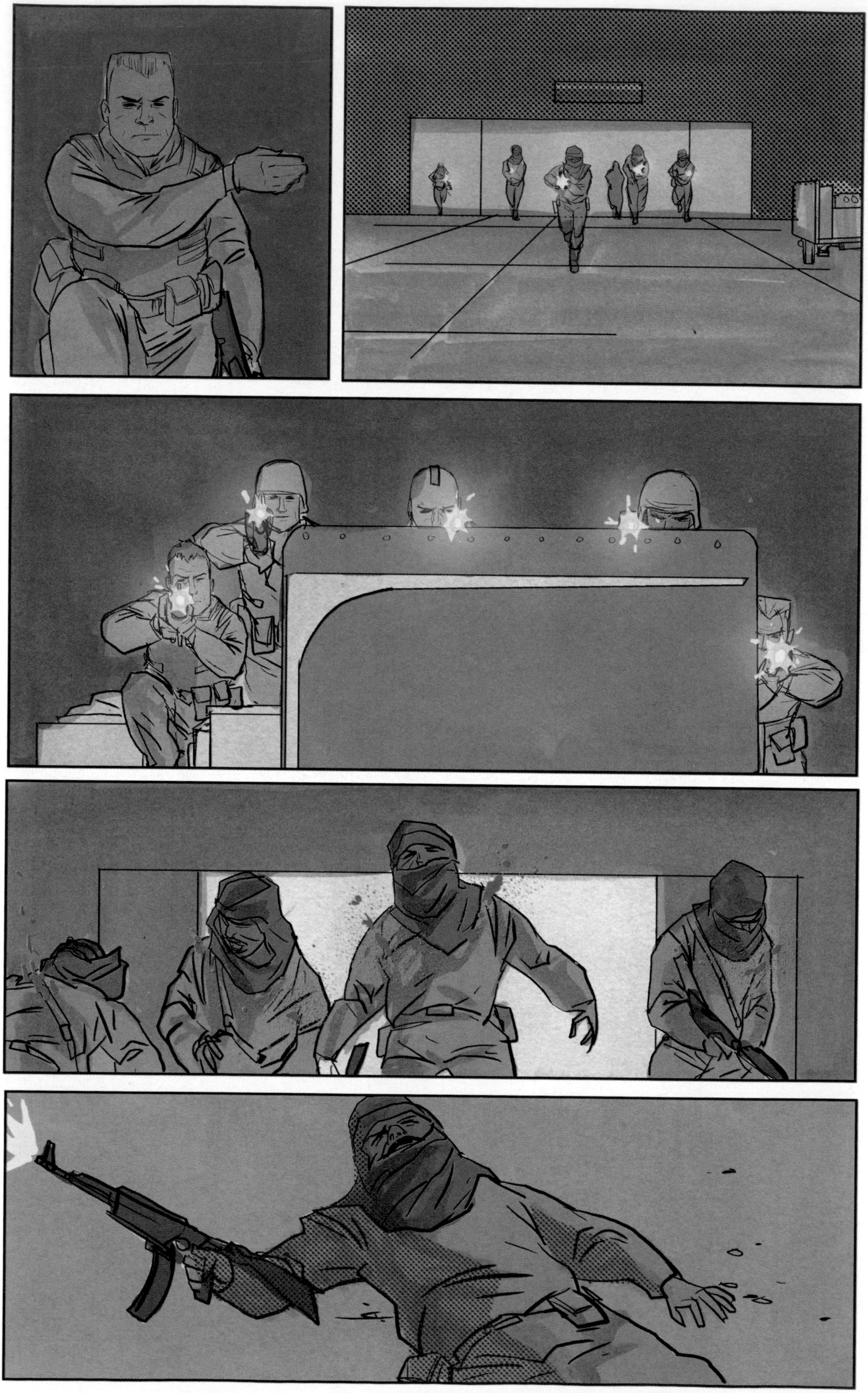

RELOADING!
GUH
GETTING KILLED TAKES ONLY A **SECOND...**
UUUH-- SOR...
S-SORRY.
...BUT IN THE EYES YOU SEE ANOTHER TRUTH--
--DYING TAKES **FOREVER.**
WE'RE GETTING YOU **HOME.**
I HAD SAID THOSE **SAME WORDS** TO SO MANY OF MY MEN. EVEN IF YOU DIED IN SOME DESERT SHITHOLE HALF A WORLD AWAY--**EVERYBODY GOES HOME.** AND IT WAS ALWAYS **TRUE.**
BUT NOT THIS TIME. I'VE ALWAYS HOPED THAT HE WAS GONE BEFORE MY LIE REACHED HIS EARS. I NEVER SAID THOSE WORDS AGAIN.

CLEAR.
GATHER THEIR AK'S. MOVE OUT.
THE BEST WE COULD DO FOR OUR COMRADE WAS STILL SHIT.
I REMEMBER SOME OF THE MEN SAYING SOME PRAYERS. I DON'T HAVE THOSE WORDS.
I HOPE HE NEVER HEARD ME.
I HOPE HE FORGAVE ME.

MOST EVERYTHING A SOLDIER DEPENDS ON HAD TOTALLY BROKEN DOWN. I WONDERED IF THEY THOUGHT I FAILED THEM, BUT THERE WAS NO TIME FOR ANY OF THAT CRAP.
WE'RE MOVING OUT RIGHT NOW.
"LEAVE NO MAN BEHIND".
MORE ANCIENT HISTORY FOR THE SAND.
BURY YOUR UNIFORMS AND WEAPONS. PUT ON THE CIVVIES AND GET COMFORTABLE WITH THEIR AK'S. WE'RE GOING NATIVE.
WHAT'S THE PLAN?
LAY LOW. GET TO A PORT. FIND A **BOAT.**

WE'RE ON OUR OWN.
THAT'S HOW IT BEGAN. WE PUT OUR BACKS TO THE UTTER DESTRUCTION WE HAD WROUGHT AND STARTED FOR **HOME**...NEVER GUESSING THE **HELL** WE WERE DESCENDING INTO.

CHAPTER TWO
"Red Sky At Morning"

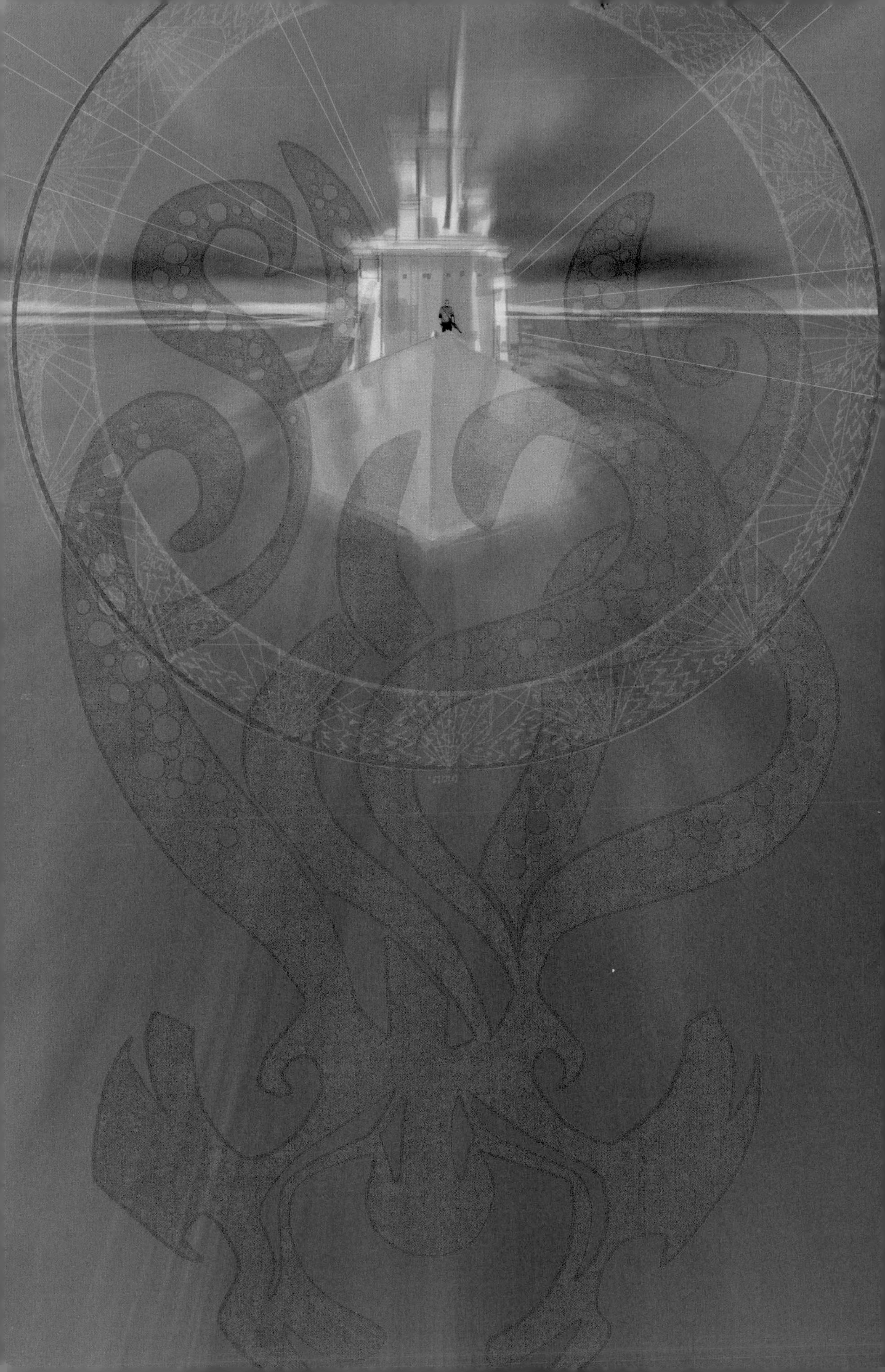

ISN'T MY MOM SHARING THE WATER? HOW COME THEY DON'T TRUST US?
IT'S COMPLICATED. NOBODY EVER THOUGHT ABOUT WATER UNTIL IT STOPPED COMING OUT OF THEIR FAUCETS.
HOW COME MY MOM SENT ME AWAY?
THAT'S COMPLICATED TOO.
AS LONG AS HE'S HERE WITH ME--MY SON IS IN DANGER. YOU MUST TAKE HIM DOWN TO YOUR FARM. IT'S THE ONLY WAY I CAN MAKE SURE HE'S SAFE.
BUT--
I'M TRAPPED HERE NOW. HE DOESN'T HAVE TO BE.
I THINK WE'RE FAR ENOUGH AWAY NOW TO LET YOU DOWN. BESIDES, YOU'RE GETTING KIND OF HEAVY.
HOW COME SHE DIDN'T COME WITH US?

SHE'S GOT A LOT OF RESPONSIBILITY UNTIL YOUR FATHER RETURNS.
HOW LONG DO I HAVE TO BE GONE?
AS LONG AS SHE SAYS. YOU DIDN'T DO ANYTHING WRONG, SON. YOUR MOTHER JUST HAS A LOT ON HER PLATE RIGHT NOW.
SO SHE'S WORRIED SOMETHING COULD HAPPEN AT HOME?
EXACTLY. BOY, YOU DON'T MISS MUCH, DO YOU?
YOU'RE JUST AS SMART AS YOUR OLD MAN.

THE QUIET MONTHS FOLLOWING OUR ESCAPE FROM THE AIRPORT WERE SPENT MAKING THIS TUB SEAWORTHY. WE AVOIDED OUR ENEMIES AND EVEN MADE SOME FRIENDS. THEY HELPED US ESCAPE AND THEIR ONLY PRICE WAS GETTING THEIR FAMILIES OUT.
OUR LOCAL ALLIES BARTERED FOR THE MATERIAL WE NEEDED-- AND MY MEN STOLE THE REST.
IF WE COULD REACH WESTERN EUROPE, I WOULD HAVE SEEN MY FAMILY BY THE END OF THAT FIRST YEAR... BUT THAT NIGHT CHANGED MY FORTUNE **FOREVER**.
LOOK! THAT'S A GOOD OMEN, RIGHT?
MONTHS HAD PASSED SINCE THE CHINESE STRIKE IN SPACE...
HNH.
...AND THE PIECES WERE STILL FALLING.
DIST • 32.673 MI 89 43

THAT ONE--IS **BAD** LUCK.
HOW DO YOU KNOW?
OH, SHIT!
ARE THEY STILL ALIVE UP THERE?
NO. ANYONE ON THE SPACE STATION FROZE TO DEATH MONTHS AGO IF THEY COULDN'T REBOOT THE SYSTEMS AFTER...
DAMN!
WHAT!?
GO TELL FORTUNATO TO CUT THE ENGINES AND LIGHTS! **MOVE.**
BEFORE WE PUT TO SEA I SPENT EVERY NIGHT WONDERING IF A BOAT WAS THE RIGHT DECISION.
THAT WAS THE MOMENT I KNEW IT WAS NOT.

I COULDN'T TELL IF THEY WERE SYRIANS, OR EGYPTIANS OR IF THEY WERE SUNNI OR SHIA. JUST THAT THEY WERE DEAD.
AND NOT FOR VERY LONG.

HERE'S THE SITUATION. BODIES IN THE WATER. OIL SLICK. BOTH FRESH.
SHIT. THE WEATHER'S BEEN FINE... PIRATES?
WE'LL LOSE THE DARKNESS SOON.
WE COULD TURN BACK--
NO! WE CANNOT! IF WE ARE FOUND WITH YOU THEY WILL KILL MY ENTIRE FAMILY! YOU'VE SEEN WHAT THEY DO TO ANYONE THAT HELPS AMERICANS.
YEAH, YEAH. WE'VE SEEN WHAT HAPPENS TO AMERICANS, TOO--
DOESN'T MATTER. THERE'S NO GOING BACK. BY NOW, THE SHIPS WE SABOTAGED HAVE BEEN DISCOVERED. WE KNOCKED DOWN A HORNETS NEST BEHIND US.
HAMZA, IS THERE ANYWHERE WE CAN LAY LOW UNTIL THE SUN SETS AGAIN TOMORROW?
NOT LIKELY. AND IF WE BEACH HER--WE WILL NEVER GET HER BACK INTO THE WATER.
SYRIA
Aleppo
LEBANON
EGYPT
Cairo
GREECE
ALBANIA
BULGARIA
Bucharest
Constanta
Ionian Sea
NO ARGUING THAT. OK, THEN. MOVE US FURTHER AWAY FROM LAND, BUT KEEP US ON COURSE. BEST SPEED. LIGHTS OUT.
THE MOMENT I PUT US ON THIS BOAT I TRAPPED US.

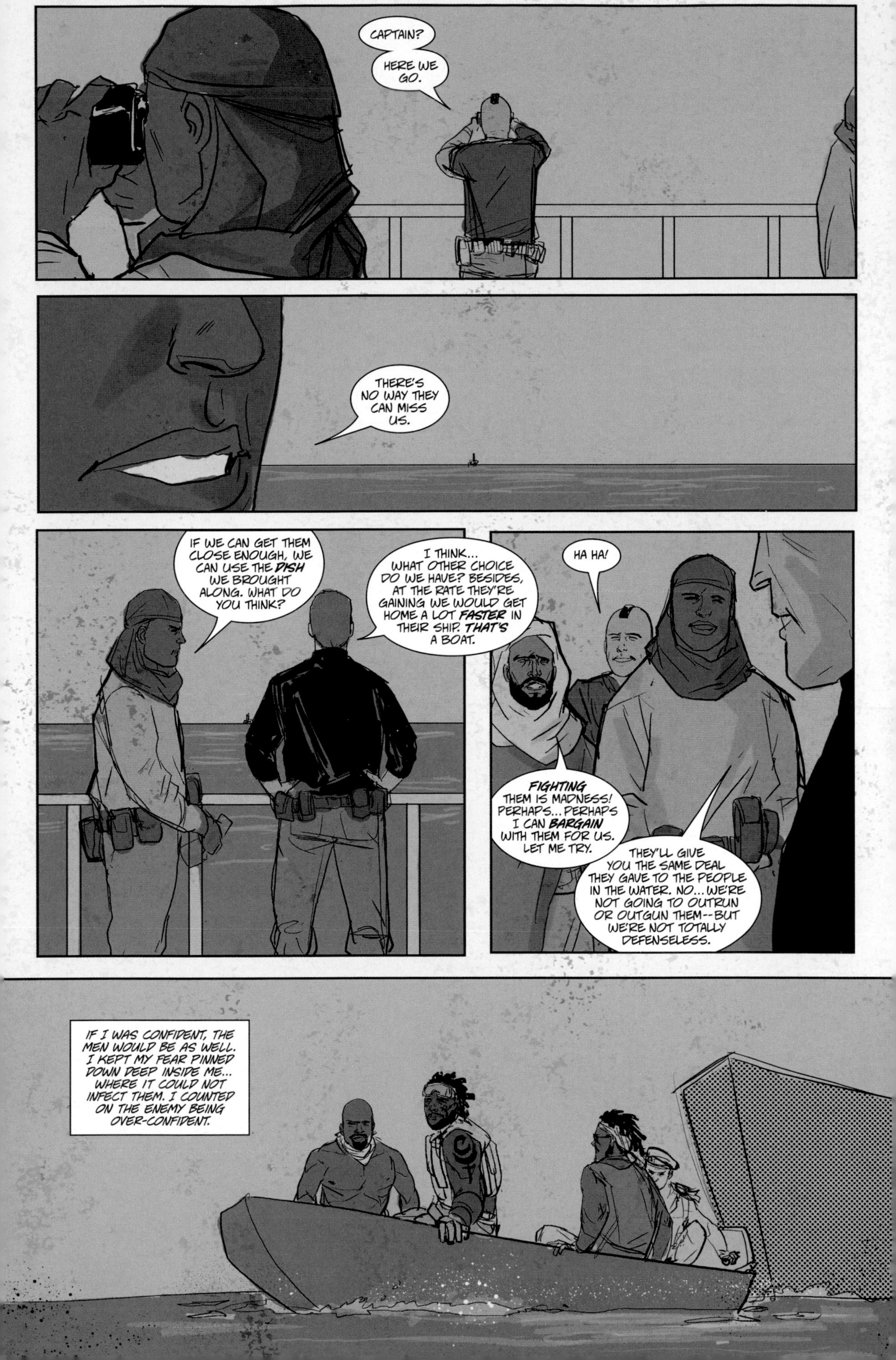
CAPTAIN?
HERE WE GO.
THERE'S NO WAY THEY CAN MISS US.
IF WE CAN GET THEM CLOSE ENOUGH, WE CAN USE THE DISH WE BROUGHT ALONG. WHAT DO YOU THINK?
I THINK... WHAT OTHER CHOICE DO WE HAVE? BESIDES, AT THE RATE THEY'RE GAINING WE WOULD GET HOME A LOT FASTER IN THEIR SHIP. THAT'S A BOAT.
HA HA!
FIGHTING THEM IS MADNESS! PERHAPS... PERHAPS I CAN BARGAIN WITH THEM FOR US. LET ME TRY.
THEY'LL GIVE YOU THE SAME DEAL THEY GAVE TO THE PEOPLE IN THE WATER. NO... WE'RE NOT GOING TO OUTRUN OR OUTGUN THEM--BUT WE'RE NOT TOTALLY DEFENSELESS.
IF I WAS CONFIDENT, THE MEN WOULD BE AS WELL. I KEPT MY FEAR PINNED DOWN DEEP INSIDE ME... WHERE IT COULD NOT INFECT THEM. I COUNTED ON THE ENEMY BEING OVER-CONFIDENT.

YOU'RE LETTING THEM COME ABOARD?!
CAN'T STOP THEM. NOW GET BELOW DECK. FORTUNATO, GET INTO POSITION ATOP THE WHEEL HOUSE. DON'T WAIT FOR MY CUE.
RIGHT.
TELL THE MEN IN THE WHEELHOUSE TO KEEP MOVING US INTO RANGE. SLOWLY.
YES, SIR.
PERMISSION TO COME ABOARD?
GRANTED.
THESE ARE DANGEROUS WATERS, CAPTAIN.
ARE THEY? BUT YOU'RE THE FIRST VESSEL WE'VE COME ACROSS.
THAT IS VERY FORTUNATE.

YOU HERE TO PROTECT US?
INDEED. OUR NAVY IS SEARCHING EVERY VESSEL IN OUR TERRITORIAL WATERS.
THIS IS TO ENSURE SAFE CONDUCT FOR EVERYONE. BRING YOUR CREW ONTO THE DECK FOR INSPECTION.
I WASN'T AWARE THERE WERE ANY TERRITORIAL WATERS THAT EXTENDED SO FAR FROM LAND.
YOU ARE MISTAKEN.
ARE YOU SURE THERE ISN'T SOME KIND OF ARRANGEMENT WE COULD MAKE? PERHAPS I COULD PAY YOU FOR SAFE CONDUCT THROUGH THIS OBVIOUSLY DANGEROUS TERRITORY?
YOU THINK A SIMPLE BRIBE CAN PAY FOR AN INCURSION INTO OUR WATERS? THERE IS NOTHING YOU HAVE THAT WE CANNOT TAKE FROM YOU. TELL YOUR CREW TO COME ONTO THE DECK AND LEAVE THEIR WEAPONS BELOW.
IF YOU JUMP OVERBOARD THIS SECOND, YOU MIGHT LIVE.

ARE YOU OUT YOUR MIND? HAVE YOU NOT LOOKED BEHIND ME?
PERHAPS YOU SHOULD LOOK AGAIN.
SORRY YOU COULDN'T WORK OUT A DEAL.

NON-LETHAL WEAPONRY HAS TREMENDOUS ADVANTAGES IN THE RIGHT SITUATIONS.
WHAT ARE YOU DOING?
THESE ARE DANGEROUS WATERS.
IT WAS AMAZING WHAT HAMZA FOUND ON THE BLACK MARKET AFTER AMERICA WITHDREW. LIKE THE MICROWAVE SYSTEM WE STRIPPED FROM THAT STRYKER COMBAT VEHICLE.
GET OFF!-- URK!
BLAM!
UNH
DROP THE BOAT! CUT 'EM LOOSE!

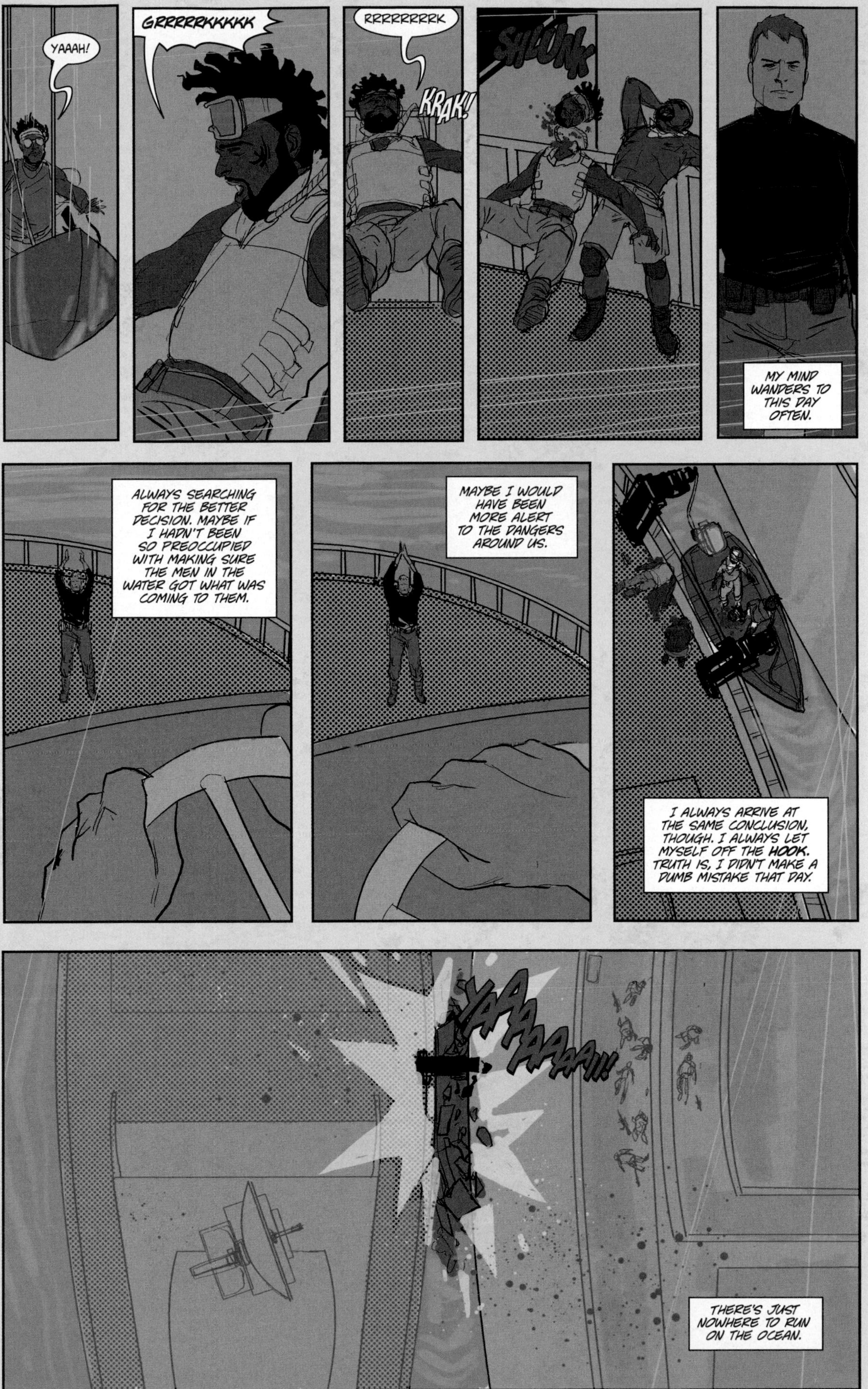
YAAAH!
GRRRRRKKKKK
RRRRRRRRK
KRAK!!
SHLUNK
MY MIND WANDERS TO THIS DAY OFTEN.
ALWAYS SEARCHING FOR THE BETTER DECISION. MAYBE IF I HADN'T BEEN SO PREOCCUPIED WITH MAKING SURE THE MEN IN THE WATER GOT WHAT WAS COMING TO THEM.
MAYBE I WOULD HAVE BEEN MORE ALERT TO THE DANGERS AROUND US.
I ALWAYS ARRIVE AT THE SAME CONCLUSION, THOUGH. I ALWAYS LET MYSELF OFF THE HOOK. TRUTH IS, I DIDN'T MAKE A DUMB MISTAKE THAT DAY.
YAAAAAAAAA!!!
THERE'S JUST NOWHERE TO RUN ON THE OCEAN.

GET READY TO BOARD. THEY'RE DOWN, BUT NOT OUT.
SUB SURFACING! **INCOMING!** TORPEDO IN THE WATER!
I LET FAMILIES ON BOARD. HOW COULD I HAVE BEEN SO STUPID?
NOWHERE TO RUN.

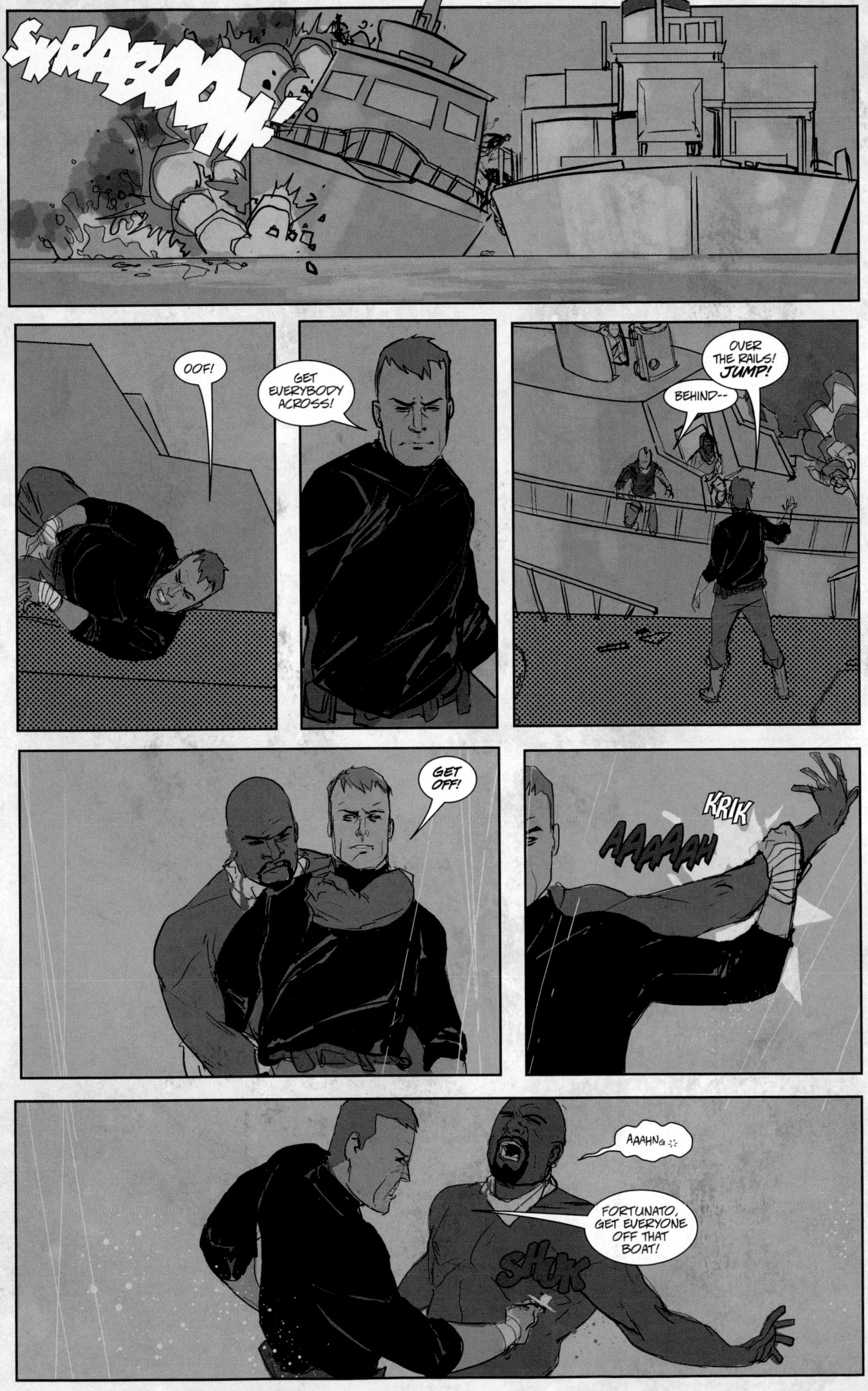
SKRABOOM!
OOF!
GET EVERYBODY ACROSS!
OVER THE RAILS! JUMP!
BEHIND--
GET OFF!
KRIK
AAAAAH
AAAHNG
FORTUNATO, GET EVERYONE OFF THAT BOAT!
SHUK

ONE OF THE ONLY THINGS I DID RIGHT THAT DAY WAS KNOWING WHEN I WAS BEAT.
I KNEW THAT SUB WAS PREPARING TO FIRE ON THEIR OWN BOAT AND BOTH THESE SHIPS WOULD BE ON THE WAY TO THE BOTTOM.
THEY WERE GOING TO KILL US...
BLAM! BLAM!
GAH!
VOOOM!
...BUT I WAS GOING TO TAKE THEM DOWN WITH ME.

EMERGENCY DIVE! DIVE!
HOLD FAST!
SKRREEEEEEEEEEEEUUUUUUNNCHK
IT WAS DEAD QUIET FOR I DON'T KNOW HOW LONG. THEN THE SCREAMING STARTED. THE MEN, THE SHIPS...

...AND THE WOMEN.
GRAB EMERGENCY GEAR AND GET OVERBOARD! NOW!
IF ANYONE CAN HEAR ME-- SWIM TO ME! I HAVE A RAFT!
HELP US!
PLEASE!
FUCKING HELL! FOLLOW MY--
...VOICE.
PRAISE ALLAH!
HELP!
WHERE'S IT--WHERE'S IT LOCKED FROM?!
THE KEY! THE CAPTAIN HAD THE KEY!
ARE OUR HUSBANDS UP THERE? FIND MY HUSBAND! PLEASE!
GET US OUT!
GET BACK!

IT'S THE DAMNDEST THING. I DON'T REMEMBER FIRING. I THINK I DID. WHAT DOES IT MATTER?
I KNOW WORDS PASSED BETWEEN US... THEIR LAST WORDS ON EARTH... FOR THE LIFE OF ME, I CAN'T REMEMBER WHAT THE HELL THEY WERE.
SORRY.
WHAT THE HELL WERE YOU DOING BACK THERE? WHAT DID YOU FIND?
NOTHING.
I DIDN'T FIND ANYTHING.
GIMME YOUR HAND.
HELL, WE'RE SCREWED NOW.

WHATEVER IT IS, I'M NOT INTERESTED, HULL.
DON'T BE SO SURE, BITCH.
YOU'RE GOING TO NEED TO START CHANGING YOUR TONE WITH ME.
NOBODY'S HURT... WELL, THAT AIN'T EXACTLY TRUE.
OH GOD!
YOUR BABY-SITTER WENT AND GOT HIMSELF KILLED, BUT YOUR BOY AIN'T HURT. NOT YET... AND IF YOU COOPERATE WITH US NOTHING BAD WILL HAPPEN.
I'VE LOST HIM. I'VE LOST OUR SON. STOP. BREATHE. DON'T PANIC. DON'T SHOW THIS MAN FEAR.
WELL, AIN'T YOU GONNA SAY SOMETHING?

I HEAR YOU PERFECTLY.
WHAT DO YOU...
HE'S COMING BACK.
WHAT DO... YOU KNOW OF MY HUSBAND? BECAUSE IF ANY HARM COMES TO MY SON: HE WILL VISIT IT UPON YOU TENFOLD. IT'S CLEAR YOU HAVEN'T THOUGHT THIS THROUGH VERY WELL. IT'S NOT TOO LATE. THINK THINGS OVER TONIGHT.
YOUR FARMS WON'T GET ANOTHER DROP OF WATER UNTIL I SEE MY SON SAFELY INSIDE THIS HOUSE.

THE MEAGER EMERGENCY SUPPLIES ON THE RAFT WERE RATIONED. WE GOT THROUGH SEVERAL FREEZING NIGHTS...
...AND BRUTALLY OPPRESSIVE DAYS. THE DAY OUR WATER RAN DRY WE KNEW IT WAS THE END...
...BUT THAT NIGHT THE HORIZON BURNED, SHOWING US THE WAY OFF THE WATER.
IN MY...WEAKER MOMENTS SINCE THEN...I'VE WONDERED IF IT WOULD HAVE BEEN BETTER NOT TO HAVE SEEN THE VOLCANO THAT NIGHT.
BUT NONE OF US GET TO CHOOSE OUR FATE. JUST STAND UP TO IT WHEN THE TIME COMES.
STILL, MAKING IT TO THE ISLAND MEANT A CHANCE TO STAY ALIVE...AT LEAST A WHILE LONGER.
...WATER.
NO! WAIT...FOR DAWN...WE'LL GO TOGETHER.

STOP.
THE VOICE I USED TO COMMAND SOLDIERS HAD NOT CHANGED--BUT THE MEN NO LONGER HAD THE MIND TO HEAR ORDERS.
THE OCEAN HAD TAKEN MY WILL TO EVEN STAND. MY BODY SANK INTO THE SAND.
HELL WITH HIM.
I WAS DEAD TO THE WORLD UNTIL THAT UNMISTAKABLE SMELL. BLOOD. IN AN INSTANT--I WAS ALIVE AGAIN.
GET UP, STAY QUIET.

WE'RE IN TROUBLE.

CHAPTER THREE
"Nobody's Invincible"

THE OCEAN LEFT ME DEHYDRATED, STARVED, AND EXHAUSTED.
FINALLY, I WAS HUNTED.
I KNEW OUR ONLY WEAPON HAD JUST ONE ROUND IN THE CLIP AND ONE IN THE CHAMBER. WHILE WE WERE ON THE OCEAN I HAD OBSESSED OVER WHICH OF US WOULD GET THE EASY WAY OUT.

TWO ROUNDS. I HAD TO WAIT FOR POINT BLANK SHOTS.
YOU GO HIGH, I'LL GO LOW.
LET HIM GO!
HE WAS POWERFUL, CONFIDENT, AND POSSESSED EVERY PHYSICAL ADVANTAGE...
...AND HE SAW RIGHT THROUGH ME.
YAH!
NNH

NNNNGGGGGG
Время умереть!
AIIIII OH...
OH GOD!
I FIRE TWICE.
BLAM! BLAM!
CHIK
AND I MISS TWICE...OR HIS ARMOR SAVES HIM.
Вы выход? Американский?

YAAA!
HUFF!
WE STAY HERE--WE DIE.
WHAT ABOUT OUR GUY?
LET'S SEE IF WE CAN LEAD THIS MANIAC AWAY FROM HIM.

MAYBE NEXT TIME HE'LL FOLLOW ORDERS.
THAT BEACH WAS NOT THE PLACE FOR US TO MAKE OUR STAND.
HEH.
VVMMMEEE
WHAT'S "TEENY" BACK THERE GOT ON?
DON'T KNOW. NEVER SEEN ANYTHING LIKE IT BEFORE.
BEFORE WE WERE GOING TO FIGHT, WE WERE GOING TO NEED **WATER**.
532ю904567

LOOK, WE FEEL FOR YOU. THEY HAVE YOUR BOY, AND THEY KILLED BURKE. BUT, CAN'T WE JUST APPEAL TO THE STATE MILITIA? WE COULD SEND RIDERS TO ALBANY. THEY MIGHT BE ABLE TO GET YOUR SON BACK WITHOUT ANY MORE OF US DYING.
CATSKILL MOUNTAINS, NEW YORK
IT'S WORTH THE CHANCE. BUT WITH EVERYTHING THAT'S GOING ON IN THIS COUNTRY RIGHT NOW-- I DON'T THINK HELP FROM THE STATE IS LIKELY.
BETWEEN THE DISEASES, THE FIGHTING, THE FLOODING, AND GOD KNOWS WHAT ELSE--THEIR HANDS ARE FULL.
WHO EVEN KNOWS WHEN THE LAST TIME THE STATE WORKERS WERE EVEN PAID? THERE MAY NOT BE A MILITIA THIS MONTH.
WELL, I WANT TO COVER MY ASS-- THINGS MAY NOT ALWAYS BE THIS BAD, AND I DON'T WANT ANY OF WHAT WE'RE TALKING ABOUT TO COME BACK ON ME.
I AGREE. WE SHOULD SEND MEN TO ALBANY, BUT MY HUSBAND WOULD NOT WAIT FOR HELP TO ARRIVE--AND NEITHER WILL I.
HEY...UH... I'VE BEEN MEANING TO ASK...ANY WORD FROM HIM?

UNFORTUNATELY, NO. BUT I'VE NOT LOST HOPE. A MONTH AGO A BOY FROM KINGSTON RETURNED. I'M SURE HE'S ON HIS WAY BACK HERE--I CAN FEEL IT IN MY HEART.
YOU DIDN'T ASK FOR IT, BUT HERE'S A PIECE OF ADVICE FOR YOU: ANYBODY ASKS YOU ABOUT YOUR OLD MAN--TELL THEM HE GOT WORD TO YOU SOMEHOW AND THAT HE'S GOING TO BE HOME SOON.
THAT'S AN EXCELLENT IDEA. IT MIGHT BE FUN TO TELL THE SQUATTERS THAT HE'S ON THE WAY HERE AND BRINGING SOME OF HIS MEN, TOO.
SO. WHAT WILL IT BE? MAYBE NEXT TIME THESE GANGS WILL WANT SOMETHING...OR SOMEONE BELONGING TO YOU.
WHAT THE HELL. WE'LL GO BRING HULL HERE.
COULD BE A WAR.
COULD BE FUN.

MAYBE THE ARMOR IS RUSSIAN? ISRAELI?
IT MUST BE SOMEBODY'S ANSWER TO AMERICA'S COMBAT SYSTEM. ASSUME THAT IT'S SELF-POWERED...NOT HAMPERED BY THIS VISIBILITY...AND THAT IT'S LINKED TO ANY OTHER NEARBY ARMORS...
THAT'S A SCARY THOUGHT.
HOW'S THE ARM?
MISSING A PIECE.
THERE'S A DRONE UP! HE FOUND US!
SPLIT UP!
RUN!

I ENTERED THE CAVE THINKING ABOUT SETTING A TRAP.
BUT I KNEW IMMEDIATELY I WAS NOT ALONE: THE PUTRID AIR CHOKED ME.
WHO ARE YOU? WHERE'S THE MASTER?
STAY BACK!
I'LL HAVE YOU OUT OF THERE IN JUST A SECOND.
I DON'T UNDERSTAND...
IT'S A TEST! NOBODY LEAVE! IT'S A TRICK!
SOMETHING WAS WRONG WITH THOSE PEOPLE.
THE MASTER WILL KILL US IF WE LEAVE.
I'LL KILL YOU FIRST. GET MOVING.
WE'RE THE SAME NOW.
IT WAS...UNNERVING NOT KNOWING IF HE HAD TAKEN THEIR EYES...OR IF THEY HAD BLINDED THEMSELVES.

I RUN HIS SHEEP OUT OF THEIR PEN, BUT ONE OF THEM IS DIFFERENT.
SHE HAD NONE OF THE WEAR AND TEAR THAT THE OTHERS DID.
DID YOU KILL HIM?
SHE WAS IMPORTANT TO HIM...BUT HOW IMPORTANT? ENOUGH TO BE A WEAKNESS?
HER HANDS WEREN'T WORN DOWN, HER SKIN UNBROKEN.
SHE LEADS ME TO HER CAPTOR'S SECRET. ONE WORTH KILLING US FOR THE MOMENT WE STEPPED ON THE ISLAND.
THE GIRL READ MY THOUGHTS.
HE'S GOT THE BIO-KEY. IT WON'T TURN OVER WITHOUT IT. BELIEVE ME.
NO MATTER WHAT HAPPENS...I'M NOT GOING BACK INTO THAT CAVE.
I'LL JUMP INTO LAVA FIRST.

DON'T DO THAT. GO HIDE ON THE HILL FROM A SPOT YOU CAN STILL SEE THE PLANE.
IF I DON'T RETURN...LIE DOWN TONIGHT NEAR ONE OF THE FISSURES ON THE ISLAND. THE GAS IS POISONOUS. YOU WON'T WAKE UP.
WHAT ELSE CAN YOU TELL ME ABOUT HIM?
HE LAUGHS WHEN HE HURTS PEOPLE.
I TOLD MYSELF I COULDN'T SAVE HER. I HOPED I WAS WRONG.
THE PATH THE CRAZIES HAD CLEARED DIDN'T LOOK NEARLY LONG ENOUGH. IT WOULD HAVE TO DO.
HELP! CAP!

I HEARD MY FRIEND...DID MY ENEMY?
SHIT!
MY IDEA WAS NOT A GREAT ONE.
BUT LEAVING FORTUNATO HANGING THERE WAS THE ONLY IDEA I HAD AT THE TIME.
IT WOULD EITHER BE THE BREAK WE NEEDED, OR GET US BOTH KILLED.
I WAITED.

РПЫШНГРЛорл
WE WEREN'T ALONE.
7872398.76
НГЫОРЛ
I COULD FEEL IT.
65278.861
НГЫОРЛ
I WOULD BE READY.
I HATE THIS ISLAND.
76290.98

SICK OF THIS WAITING.
SHUT IT.
YOU'RE GOING TO TAKE ME TO MY SON. IF YOU DO NOT, I'LL START DUMPING POISON INTO THE WATER ON THE DAYS WE SEND IT YOUR WAY.
YOU MIGHT KILL YOUR OWN KID!
YOUR FRIENDS COULD BE HURTING HIM RIGHT NOW! HOW DO I KNOW?
FINE. I'LL TAKE YOU TO HIM. YOUR BOY IS DOWNSTATE.
IN THE CITY.

CHRIST!
SPLEK
NHN
TIE HIM UP. ALLOW ONE OF HIS MEN TO LEAVE NOW AND TELL HIS PEOPLE WE'RE COMING. WE LEAVE AT FIRST LIGHT.
WE'LL GET HIM BACK. YOU GOING TO BE OK?
BE READY FOR TOMORROW, I DON'T KNOW WHAT WE WILL FACE OUT THERE.

WHERE IS THE OTHER, AMERIKAN?
COULD THAT ARMOR'S SOFTWARE SPOT A SINGLE HIDDEN FACE IN THIS JUNGLE? I DIDN'T TAKE THE CHANCE. I DIDN'T LOOK UP UNTIL I HEARD HIM RIGHT IN FRONT OF ME.
CALL FOR HIM--
UHN!
WHUD!
THE ROCK WAS ANOTHER MISTAKE. HIS ARMOR ABSORBED TOO MUCH OF THE IMPACT.
IMPRESSIVE! I WAITED **TWO HOURS** BEFORE APPROACHING.
I WAITED **THREE** FOR YOU.
NOT MOVING FOR THAT LONG COST ME THE ADVANTAGE. I HAD TO GET BACK ON MY FEET AND GET THE BLOOD PUMPING AGAIN--**FAST**.
THREE HOURS?
SORRY, PAL.

LET'S KEEP THIS--
--BETWEEN YOU AND I.
WHOMP
GAK!
HA!
FWING
I LEARNED FROM MY MISTAKE WITH THE ROCK. HAD TO GET UNDER THE ARMOR. HAD TO DO IT QUICK.
THRAK
I HEAR SOMETHING SNAP. I WAS SURE IT WAS MY NECK.
NNG.
THUNK
THAT WAS AS SCARED AS I'VE EVER BEEN. HELP WAS NOT COMING.

NO!
HELP!
NO HELP.
UCK.
ERRK.
PENELOPE... SORRY

INSTINCTIVELY MY THUMBS GO FOR THE EYES. NOTHING. IT'S **THE END**.
THEN MY FOOT HITS **SOMETHING**.
FOR A SECOND--I HAVE **HOPE**.
YES.
SHUK
AANNGH!

HNH. UHN. NYET.
UCH
AIR EXPLODED BACK INTO ME.
THE TRAINING TOOK OVER.
SLIK
FWIP
I WAS GOING TO LIVE.
NYET!
STOP! STOP!

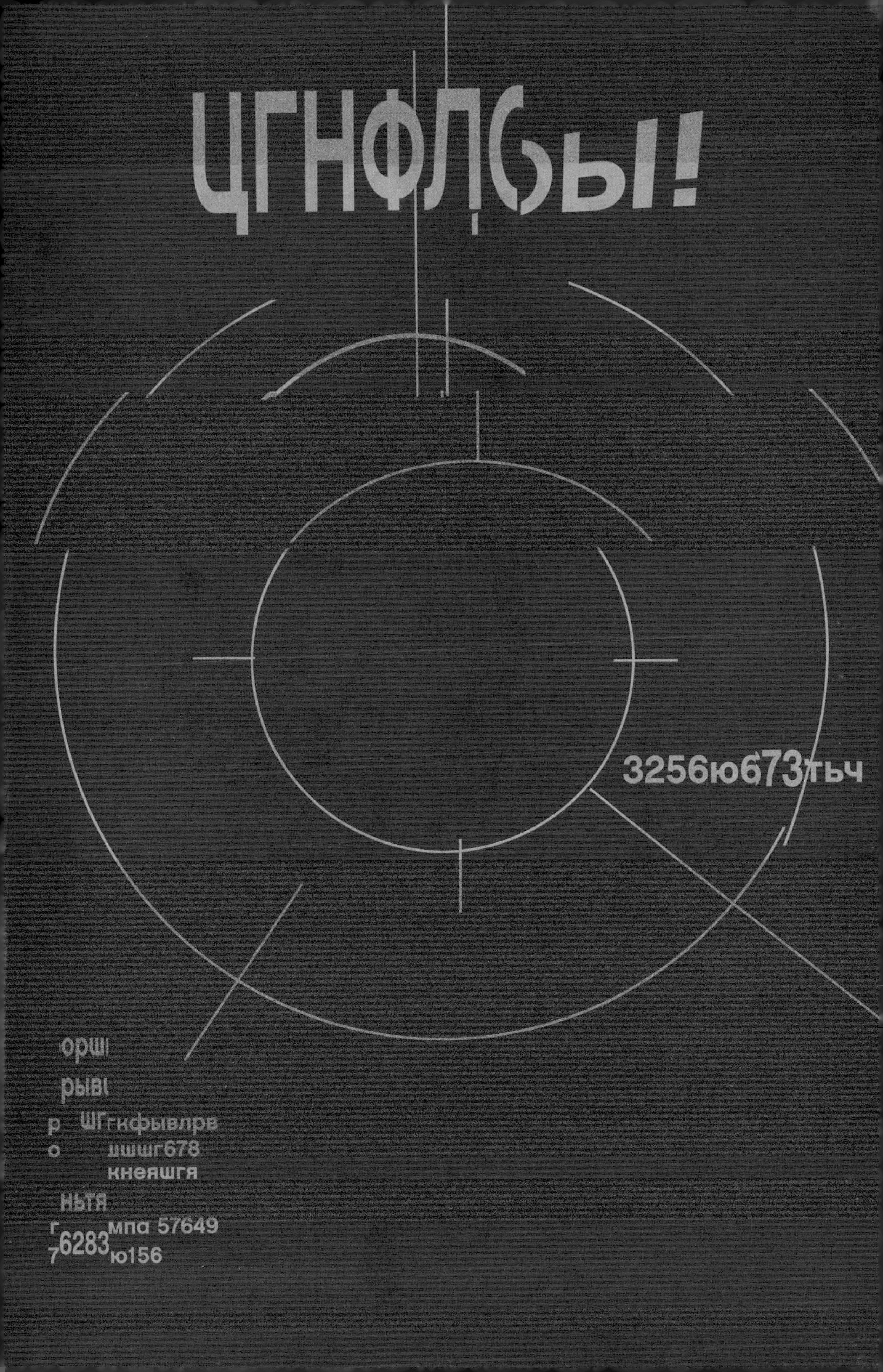
ЦГНФЛСЫ!
3256ю673тьч
орш
рыв
р ШГгкфывлрв
о шшшг678
кнеяшгя
ньтя
г мпа 57649
76283 ю156

YAAAAAKRUNK

WHO... ARE YOU?
YOU PEOPLE BRING MY FRIENDS TO ME. NOW. THE ONE CAUGHT IN THE SNARE AND THE ONE ON THE BEACH IF HE'S STILL ALIVE.
WHAT...WHAT ELSE DO YOU WANT FROM ME?
FOR STARTERS: MY KNIFE BACK.
AFTER THE ADRENALINE WORE OFF THE SHAKES AND THE PAIN RECLAIMED MY BODY. I NEEDED SLEEP. I NEEDED WATER. I NEEDED TO GET OFF THAT DAMN ISLAND.
I PALMED THE PLANE'S SMART KEY. I WANTED TO BE IN THE AIR BEFORE THOSE PEOPLE KNEW I WAS LEAVING.

WHO... WHO ARE YOU?
NOBODY.
DID SHE STAY AND WATCH HIM DIE? OR TO TRY AND HELP?
DON'T LEAVE ME LIKE THIS. NOT ALONE.
PLEASE.
MAYBE SHE KNEW THERE WASN'T ROOM FOR HER IN THE PLANE.

THE GIRL CAME DOWN OFF THE HILL SHORTLY AFTER I MADE IT BACK TO THE RUNWAY.
HATE TO SAY IT BUT THE MORE WEIGHT WE TAKE ON...THE LESS DISTANCE WE'LL TRAVEL.
DOESN'T MATTER. WE TAKE THEM ON-- WE WON'T EVEN CLEAR THOSE TREES.
I HAD TO SETTLE THE DISAGREEMENT AS TO WHO WOULD FLY... AND WHO COULD NOT.
ONE OF THEM SPITS SOMETHING AT ME THAT I CAN'T UNDERSTAND.
I'M SURE NOW THAT IT WAS A CURSE.
THE VIBRATION FROM THE ENGINE SHOOK THE PAIN FROM MY BODY.

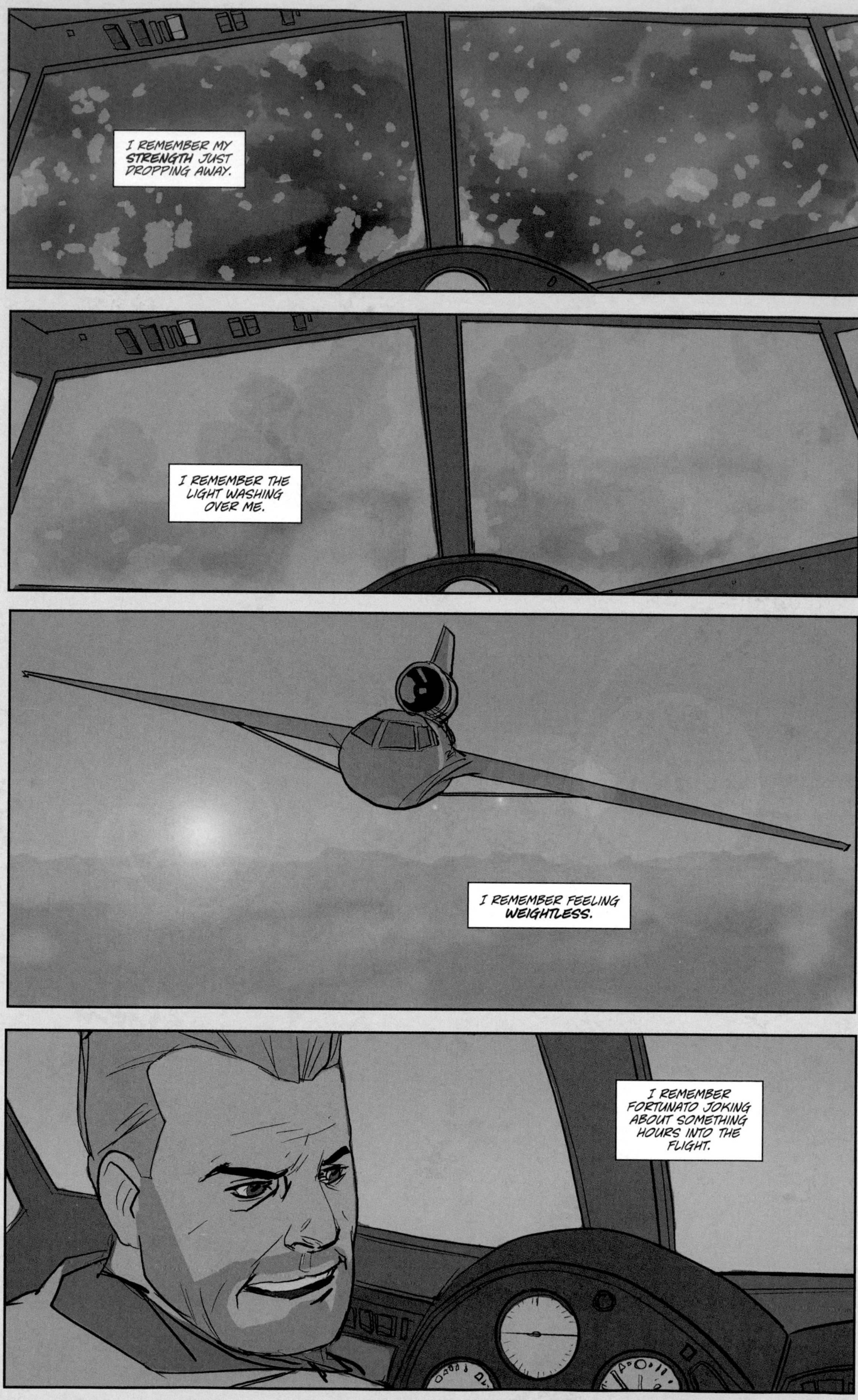
I REMEMBER MY STRENGTH JUST DROPPING AWAY.
I REMEMBER THE LIGHT WASHING OVER ME.
I REMEMBER FEELING WEIGHTLESS.
I REMEMBER FORTUNATO JOKING ABOUT SOMETHING HOURS INTO THE FLIGHT.

I REMEMBER DREAMING I FLEW ALL THE WAY HOME.
I REMEMBER REUNITING WITH MY WIFE. I REMEMBER HOLDING HER. AND I REMEMBER LAUGHING.
FORTUNATELY... I DON'T REMEMBER CRASHING.
IT HAD BEEN SUCH A BEAUTIFUL DREAM...

I AWOKE TO A NEW NIGHTMARE. HOME WAS GOING TO HAVE TO WAIT.
A LONG TIME.

CHAPTER FOUR
"That Which Does Not Kill Us"

noto

FORTUNATO TOLD ME I WAS ONLY CARRIED FOR A FEW HOURS AFTER THE CRASH. IT FELT LIKE DAYS...
THE GRINDING OF THE BONES SCREAMED THAT I WAS ALIVE.
IT'S A FLESH WOUND, YOU'LL GET ANOTHER PURPLE HEART FOR THIS.
SOMEONE'S COMING!
THE LOCALS WERE NOT HAPPY TO SEE AMERICANS MARCH INTO THEIR VILLAGE. EVEN ONES AT DEATH'S DOOR.

WELCOME TO AFRICA!
I OWE MY **SURVIVAL** AFTER THE CRASH TO MY FRIEND. BUT WHAT SAVED ME IN THE DAYS THAT FOLLOWED WAS MY **ENTERTAINMENT** VALUE.
I WAS SOMETHING TO **WAGER** ON. HOW LONG WOULD I LAST? WOULD I LOSE THE LEG BEFORE GOING? WOULD I EVEN MAKE IT THROUGH THE NIGHT?
NOBODY MADE ODDS ON MY SURVIVING.

FORTUNATO MOVED US INTO AN ABANDONED HUT. THE FORMER OCCUPANTS KILLED, OR RUN OFF LONG AGO.
THE NEXT WEEKS WERE A **HORROR** WHICH THANKFULLY I DIDN'T KEEP MUCH MEMORY OF. MY FRIENDS FOUND WHAT PASSED FOR A LOCAL DOCTOR AND HE DID THE BEST HE COULD WITH NOTHING. HE QUIT COMING AROUND. WE LEARNED LATER HE WAS MURDERED.
MY INJURIES KEPT ME DOWN FOR **MONTHS**...BUT IT WAS THE DRUG THAT KEPT ME OUT FOR **YEARS**.

BACK IN AMERICA...
HAVE YOU EVER SEEN THE CITY SO QUIET?
NEVER.
LISTEN, YOU CAN'T GET YOUR HOPES UP ABOUT ANY DEAL. THESE MEN MAY NOT GIVE UP YOUR SON.
WE'RE NOT LEAVING HERE WITHOUT HIM.
WELL, IF THIS GOES WRONG-- TRY TO STAY LOW.
NOTHING'S GOING TO GO WRONG. AND WE HAVE BURKE HERE TO EXPLAIN OUR POSITION, IF NECESSARY.

WELCOME TO NEW YORK CITY!
YOU WERE SMART TO COME BY BOAT. THE ROADS CAN BE KIND OF... DICEY.
YOU DON'T NEED THOSE MASKS ANYMORE. THEY NEVER HELPED MUCH ANYWAY.
EXIT
NY

WHERE'S MY SON? THIS IS NOT WHAT WAS AGREED TO.
HE'S HERE.
HAVE HIM BROUGHT OUT TO ME IMMEDIATELY.
YOU AIN'T EXACTLY IN THE STRONGEST NEGOTIATING POSITION, LADY.
THE ONLY THING YOU NEED TO KNOW ABOUT MY NEGOTIATING POSITION IS THAT I'M UPRIVER FROM YOU.
IF I DON'T RETURN, OR RETURN UNHAPPY EVERYONE DOWN RIVER WILL DRINK POISON.
MMPH!
I GOTTA HAND IT TO YOU, IT'S A HELL OF A PLAY...OR A HELL OF A BLUFF.
NEW YORK HAD PLENTY OF SUPER FUND SITES BEFORE IT WENT BANKRUPT AND MY NEIGHBORS WERE QUITE HAPPY TO HEAR I MAY HAVE A PLAN TO GET RID OF SOME. DO YOU HAVE SOMETHING YOU WOULD LIKE TO ADD, MR. BURKE?
SHE AIN'T LYING!

I DRANK SOME OF IT BEFORE I REALIZED WHAT IT WAS, I EVEN--
HOPEFULLY, WE UNDERSTAND EACH OTHER NOW.
YOU DON'T DISAPPOINT, LADY. HERE'S THE BEST OFFER I CAN MAKE: YOU GET YOUR SON BACK RIGHT NOW. AND WE ALL GO UPSTATE TOGETHER. IF I CAN'T GET CLEAN WATER FLOWING TO THIS CITY, IT WILL PICK SOMEBODY MEANER TO GET THE JOB DONE.
THIS DOESN'T HAVE TO BE A BAD THING. WHEN THE MONEY STARTS FLOWING AGAIN, YOU CAN BET THAT IT WILL GO WHERE THE WATER IS FIRST.
I GET MY SON RIGHT NOW--BUT I'M DONE WITH THIS MAN. I NEVER WANT TO SEE HIM AGAIN.
NEITHER DO I.
WHAT ARE YOU--
HEY, YOU HAVE TO KEEP BUSINESS PARTNERS HAPPY.

THE LEG WOULDN'T SET RIGHT. I KNEW IT WHILE THE CAST WAS STILL ON. I FOUGHT FOR MY LIFE EVERY DAY OF THAT FIRST YEAR IN NORTH AFRICA.
I SURVIVED INFECTIONS, EVEN A SPIDER BITE. I DON'T KNOW EXACTLY WHEN IT HAPPENED...I WON THE STRUGGLE TO LIVE, BUT I LET MY SANITY SLIP AWAY. THE PURPLE FLOWER DULLED THE PAIN FROM THE LEG, BUT...CAUSED **OTHER WOUNDS** TO OPEN UP.
I HAD FINALLY COME APART.
PLEASE!
HELP US!
GET US OUT OF HERE!
CAN'T BREATH!
SHUT UP.
I **HEARD** THEM DROWN OVER, AND OVER AGAIN.

I DIDN'T HAVE IT MUCH BETTER DURING THE DAY, EITHER.
IT WAS ALWAYS A MISTAKE TO ENGAGE THE OTHER VOICES.
WHY DO YOU KEEP COMING AROUND?
IT'S YOU THAT'S VISITING ME.
PERHAPS YOU'RE FEELING GUILTY? MAYBE YOU TOOK SOMETHING THATBELONGED TO ME?
HER? THE PLANE?
HA. YOU'VE GONE BATSHIT CRAZY AND STUPID.
MY LIFE! I WOULD SWITCH PLACES WITH YOU--EVEN CRIPPLED AS YOU ARE.
HAHA HAHA HAHA!
I CAN'T STAND IT! I CAN'T STAND--

HOME SLIPPED FURTHER AWAY...IT WAS A YEAR BEFORE I EVEN WENT TO TOWN.
QUIT COMPLAINING! YOU HAD TO GET UP AND MOVE AROUND. WHY NOT THE MARKET?
BECAUSE IT SMELLS OF SHIT, AND IT'S DANGEROUS.
I WAS CONVINCED THAT MY FAMILY WAS BETTER OFF WITHOUT A CRIPPLE. FORTUNATO WAITED FOR ME TO BREAK OUT OF IT. HE WAS PATIENT, BUT EVERYONE'S GOT A BREAKING POINT.
JUST BREATHE.
IT WAS A HELL OF A PLACE TO FIND A WOMAN, LET ALONE A DOCTOR. ALL SHE WANTED TO DO WAS HELP PEOPLE. THIS PLACE MADE YOU PAY FOR THAT.
THE MEEK INHERITED THIS EARTH. BUT THEY DIDN'T STAY THAT WAY FOR LONG. THE ORPHANS OF WAR WERE THE ONLY LAW.
NO, WAIT!
BLAM!
NO!
WHAT DID WE TELL YOU? NO HELPING THOSE PEOPLE!
THAT'S NOT HOW YOU HOLD A GUN, YOU LITTLE SHIT.

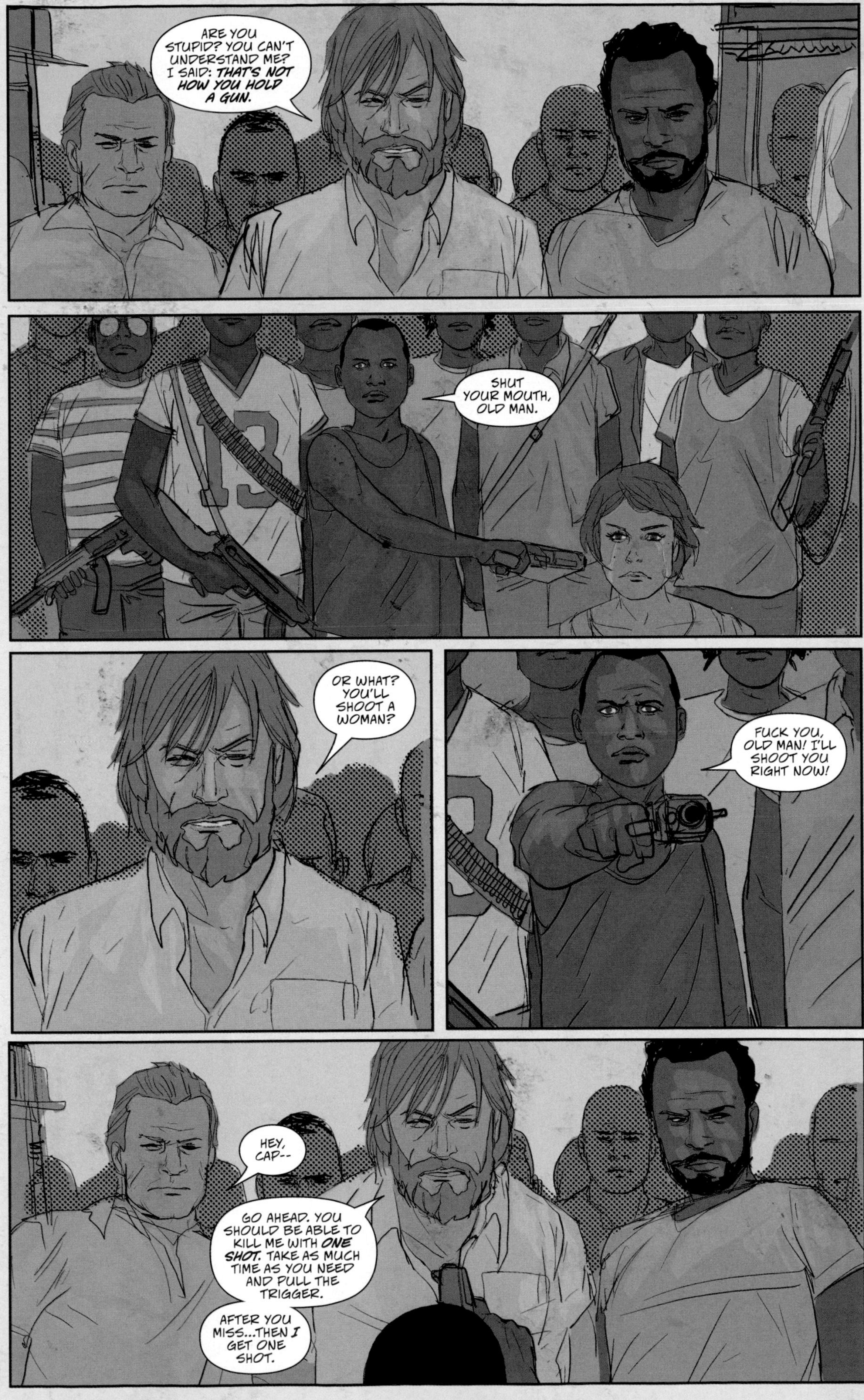
ARE YOU STUPID? YOU CAN'T UNDERSTAND ME? I SAID: THAT'S NOT HOW YOU HOLD A GUN.
SHUT YOUR MOUTH, OLD MAN.
OR WHAT? YOU'LL SHOOT A WOMAN?
FUCK YOU, OLD MAN! I'LL SHOOT YOU RIGHT NOW!
HEY, CAP--
GO AHEAD. YOU SHOULD BE ABLE TO KILL ME WITH ONE SHOT. TAKE AS MUCH TIME AS YOU NEED AND PULL THE TRIGGER.
AFTER YOU MISS...THEN I GET ONE SHOT.

I'LL PULL THE TRIGGER-- I SWEAR!
DO IT! YOU'RE NOT HITTING ME HOLDING IT LIKE THAT!
BLAM!
HOLY SHIT...

HKKKK.
UNNN.
THRAK!
NO-ACK!
SON OF A BITCH!
'TAY BACK!
DON'T.
HE IS A *WARRIOR!* WHAT'S YOUR NAME, OLD MAN?
HE'S FUCKING DEAD!
I'M NOBODY.

TEACH US TO SHOOT!
NOT HERE.
THOSE THUGS JUST MURDERED YOUR FRIEND-- HOW CAN HE BE FRIENDS WITH THEM!?
HE'S NOT BEING FRIENDLY-- HE'S GETTING TO KNOW THE ENEMY.
HE'S CRAZY.
ZZNOT THZZ LIONS.
MAYBE-- BUT YOU'RE ALIVE. HELP ME GET HIM OUT OF HERE. FIX HIS LEG.
HIS LEG IS OBVIOUSLY THE LEAST OF HIS PROBLEMS.
IF I RE-BREAK THAT LEG HERE, WITH WHAT LITTLE I HAVE, AND NO MEDICINE...IT COULD KILL HIM.
I KEEP TELLING HIM. IT'S TOO DANGEROUS TO TRY AND FIX--
WE ARE NOT LAMBS. NOR ARE WE LIONS.
HANG ON A...WHAT IS THAT?
WE'RE SURVIVORS. ALL OF US.

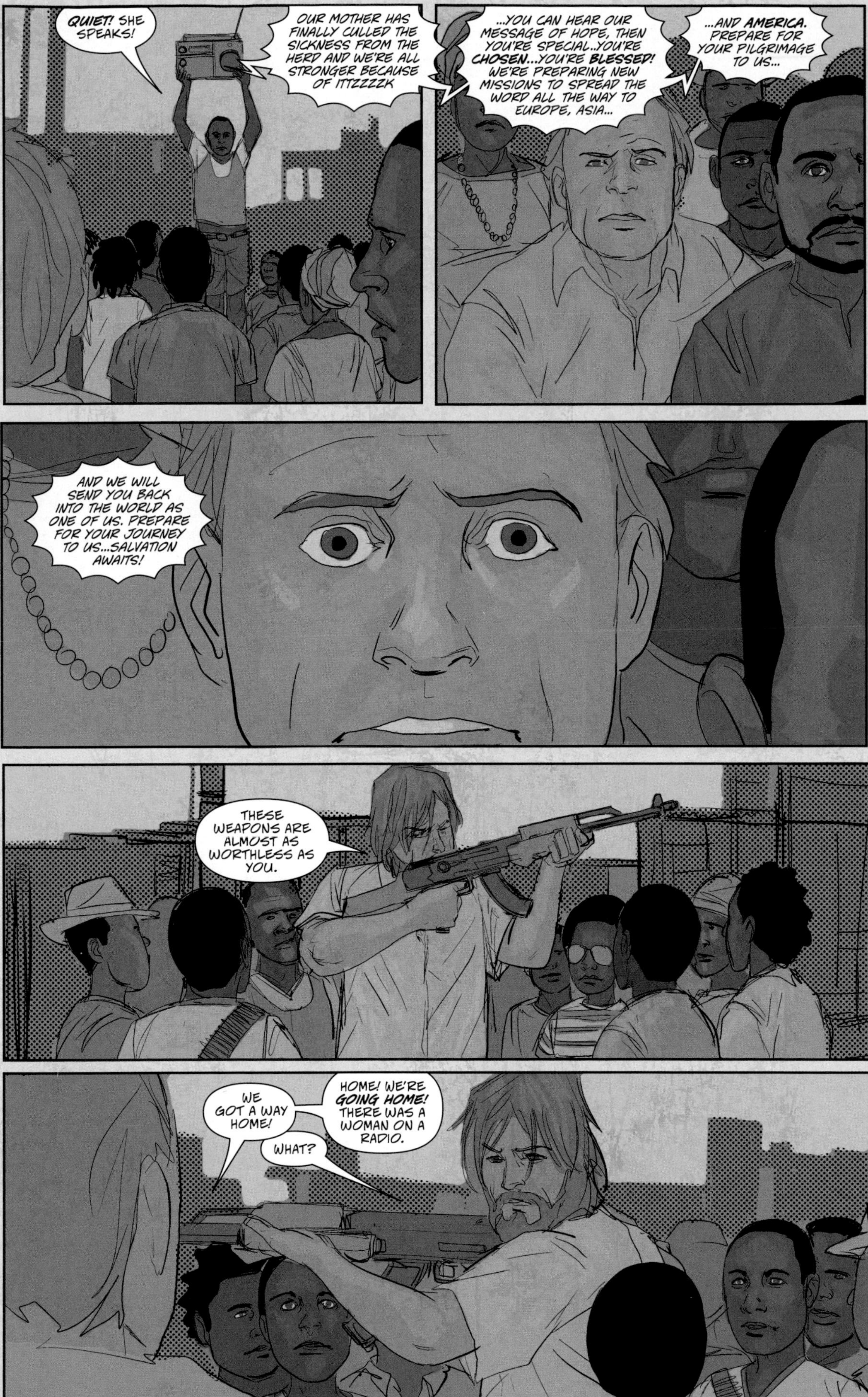
QUIET! SHE SPEAKS!
OUR MOTHER HAS FINALLY CULLED THE SICKNESS FROM THE HERD AND WE'RE ALL STRONGER BECAUSE OF ITTZZZZK
...YOU CAN HEAR OUR MESSAGE OF HOPE, THEN YOU'RE SPECIAL..YOU'RE CHOSEN...YOU'RE BLESSED! WE'RE PREPARING NEW MISSIONS TO SPREAD THE WORD ALL THE WAY TO EUROPE, ASIA...
...AND AMERICA. PREPARE FOR YOUR PILGRIMAGE TO US...
AND WE WILL SEND YOU BACK INTO THE WORLD AS ONE OF US. PREPARE FOR YOUR JOURNEY TO US...SALVATION AWAITS!
THESE WEAPONS ARE ALMOST AS WORTHLESS AS YOU.
WE GOT A WAY HOME!
HOME! WE'RE GOING HOME! THERE WAS A WOMAN ON A RADIO.
WHAT?

SHE SOUNDED A LITTLE LOOPY, BUT THEY'RE NOT AFRAID OF REVEALING THEIR POSITION WHICH MEANS THE SECURITY SITUATION MUST NOT BE AWFUL. SHE SAID THEY'RE TRAVELING ALL OVER THE WORLD--INCLUDING THE STATES.
MAYBE... MAYBE AFTER THIS NEXT RAINY SEASON...
NO, NOW. OR NEVER. THIS IS WHAT WE'VE BEEN WAITING FOR!
YOU MARCH OUT NOW, OR YOU DIE HERE AS NOTHING MORE THAN AN OLD JUNKIE.
DAMN IT-- GET OFF!
YOU'VE LOST YOUR SENSES... NOBODY NEEDED TO DIE TODAY. THAT'S ON YOU. I'M PUTTING THIS PLACE BEHIND ME. THERE'S A GROUP HEADING FOR THEIR SETTLEMENT TODAY. I'M GOING HOME.
THERE'S NO WAY HOME FROM HERE. YOU'LL DIE OUT THERE.
MAYBE... BUT THIS AIN'T A LIVING.

YOU GOT THE RIGHT IDEA, OLD MAN.
SHUT UP.
FORTUNATO, MAYBE WE CAN--
GOOD BYE.
YOU'LL CHANGE YOUR MIND. I **KNOW** IT.
YOU DON'T KNOW SHIT.
AFTER FORTUNATO LEFT I DIDN'T DREAM ABOUT THE DROWNING WOMEN ANYMORE.
THE CRAZY RUSSIAN STOPPED COMING AROUND. MY FALLEN COMRADES STOPPED HAUNTING ME. I DREAMT ONLY OF **HOME**. AND THAT WAS MUCH **WORSE**.

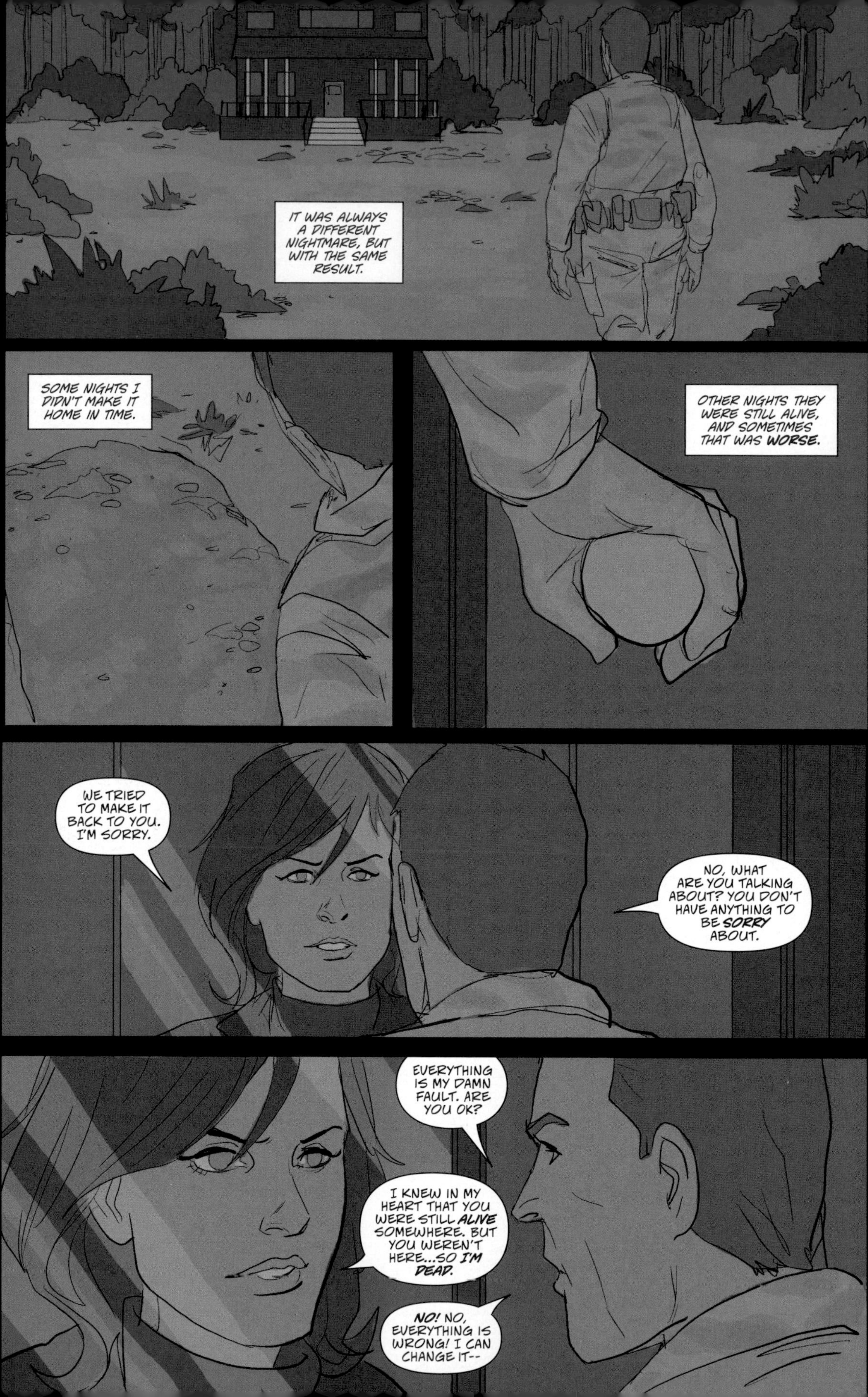
IT WAS ALWAYS A DIFFERENT NIGHTMARE, BUT WITH THE SAME RESULT.
SOME NIGHTS I DIDN'T MAKE IT HOME IN TIME.
OTHER NIGHTS THEY WERE STILL ALIVE, AND SOMETIMES THAT WAS WORSE.
WE TRIED TO MAKE IT BACK TO YOU. I'M SORRY.
NO, WHAT ARE YOU TALKING ABOUT? YOU DON'T HAVE ANYTHING TO BE SORRY ABOUT.
EVERYTHING IS MY DAMN FAULT. ARE YOU OK?
I KNEW IN MY HEART THAT YOU WERE STILL ALIVE SOMEWHERE. BUT YOU WEREN'T HERE...SO I'M DEAD.
NO! NO, EVERYTHING IS WRONG! I CAN CHANGE IT--

WAIT! WHERE'S TERRENCE? WHERE'S OUR SON?
AND WHO'S WITH YOU? ARE YOU OK? I CAN'T SEE YOU. ARE YOU STILL THERE?
PLEASE JUST GO. WE'RE ALL DEAD, AND YOU DON'T BELONG HERE.
THIS ISN'T RIGHT!

AH!
I WASN'T SCARED OF DYING.
I WAS AFRAID TO KEEP MOVING.
I WAS SCARED OF HOME.
NOT JUST OF HOW I WOULD FIND MY FAMILY--BUT OF HOW THEY WOULD FIND **ME**.
I HAD BEEN RIGHT ABOUT ONE THING, THOUGH...
THESE BONES WOULDN'T GET ME HOME.

THWAK THWAK THUCK
NNNNG
HA. AH. AH. HUNH.
I CHANGED IT ALL THAT NIGHT.
I WAS NOT GOING TO STOP MOVING.
I WASN'T SCARED ANYMORE.

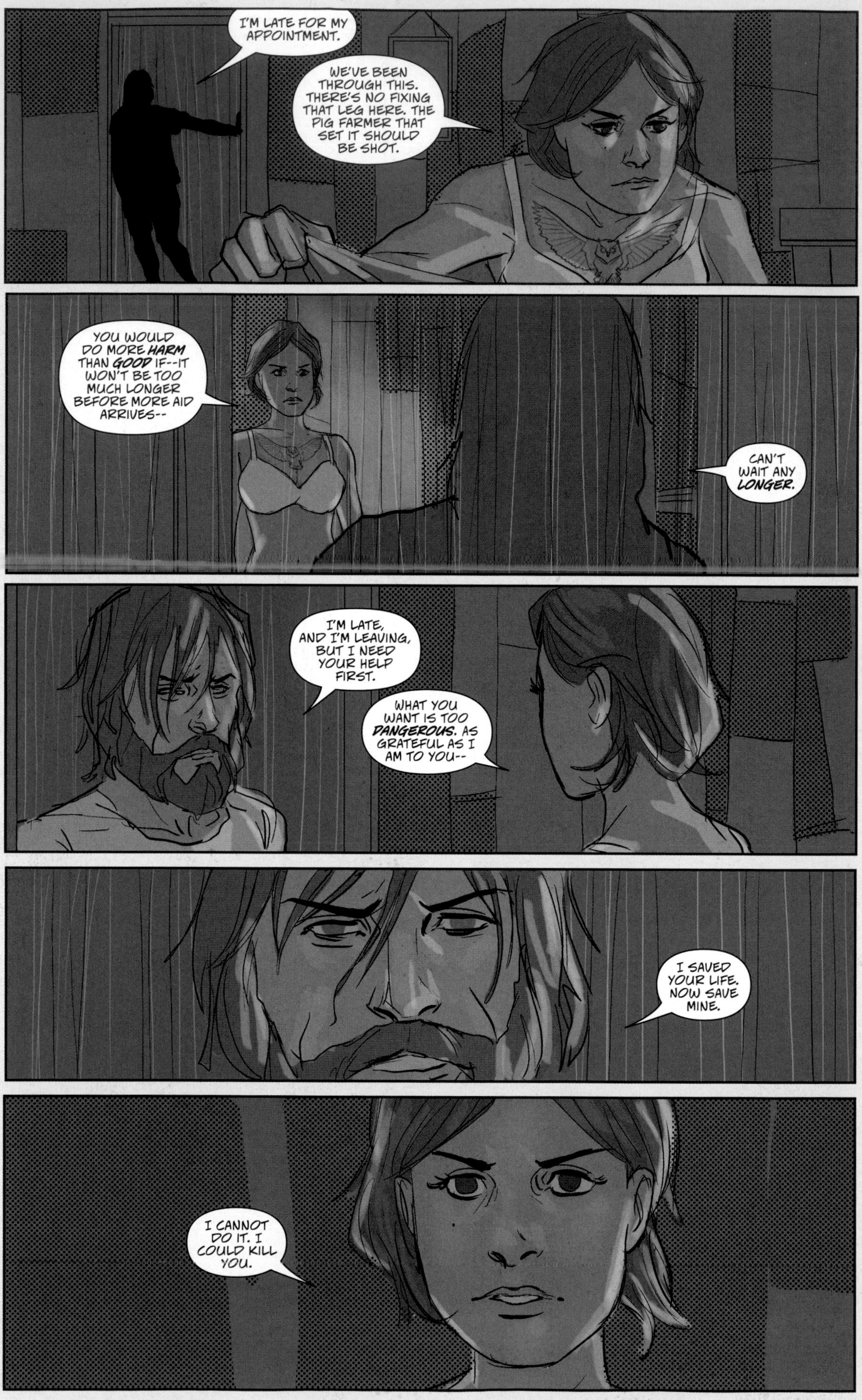
I'M LATE FOR MY APPOINTMENT.
WE'VE BEEN THROUGH THIS. THERE'S NO FIXING THAT LEG HERE. THE PIG FARMER THAT SET IT SHOULD BE SHOT.
YOU WOULD DO MORE **HARM** THAN **GOOD** IF--IT WON'T BE TOO MUCH LONGER BEFORE MORE AID ARRIVES--
CAN'T WAIT ANY **LONGER.**
I'M LATE, AND I'M LEAVING, BUT I NEED YOUR HELP FIRST.
WHAT YOU WANT IS TOO **DANGEROUS.** AS GRATEFUL AS I AM TO YOU--
I SAVED YOUR LIFE. NOW SAVE MINE.
I CANNOT DO IT. I COULD KILL YOU.

I KNOW. THAT'S WHY I STARTED FOR YOU.
LET'S GO, DOC, I DON'T HAVE ALL NIGHT.
THERE ARE WORSE THINGS THAN DEATH, AND I HAD SURVIVED THEM. I HAD FINALLY RIGHTED MYSELF, AND WAS ON COURSE FOR HOME.

CHAPTER FIVE
"Red Sky At Night"

MY LEG HAD HEALED, AND MY MIND WAS CLEAR. TO PROVE IT, I CONQUERED THE MOUNTAIN. THOSE DAMNED VOICES WERE WAITING FOR ME AT THE PEAK.
I LET THEM SPEAK TO ME WHILE I RESTED.
BOOP.
CAN YOU OVERCOME THE EVIL OF THIS WORLD BY YOURSELF? COULD YOUR FAMILY SURVIVE WITHOUT YOU? WE TAKE CARE OF OUR BROTHERS AND SISTERS. WE FEED, CLOTHE, AND PROTECT EACH OTHER.
THE WOMAN ON THE WIRELESS MADE IT SOUND LIKE SHE WAS BROADCASTING FROM SHANGRI-LA. WHICH WAS OF COURSE THE POINT. AND SHE WAS SUCCESSFUL: THE ROADS WERE CLOGGED WITH PILGRIMS SEEKING SALVATION THROUGH HER.
TRAFFIC WAS ALWAYS ONE WAY.
I'M YOUR SISTER, AND I CALL MY FAMILY HOME NOW! YOU DON'T NEED TO BE A DOCTOR OR ENGINEER TO BE A PART OF OUR NEW SOCIETY.
IT WAS TIME TO LEAVE THE WAR BEHIND, BUT I WAS NOT GOING HOME WITHOUT MY FRIEND.
HE FOLLOWED THE VOICES AND HAD NOT BEEN SEEN OR HEARD FROM AGAIN. I WAS DETERMINED TO FIND HIM SO THAT WE COULD FINISH THE JOURNEY TOGETHER.

JUST TO BE CLEAR: I'M MARCHING RIGHT INTO A TRAP--AND YOU WANT TO GO WITH ME?
IT'S A RISK WORTH TAKING IF THERE ARE REALLY SHIPS HEADING TO EUROPE OR AMERICA.
NO ARGUMENT. HAVE YOU SPOKEN TO HER?
I DID WHAT I HAD TO DO FOR THE PEOPLE HERE. NOW I NEED TO MAKE SURE THE GIRL IS SAFE.
I'M READY TO LEAVE, TOO. BUT WE MIGHT HAVE SOME TROUBLE FROM YOUR MEN.
WE KNOW YOU ARE PLANNING TO LEAVE. PLEASE, LET US WALK WITH YOU!
NO.

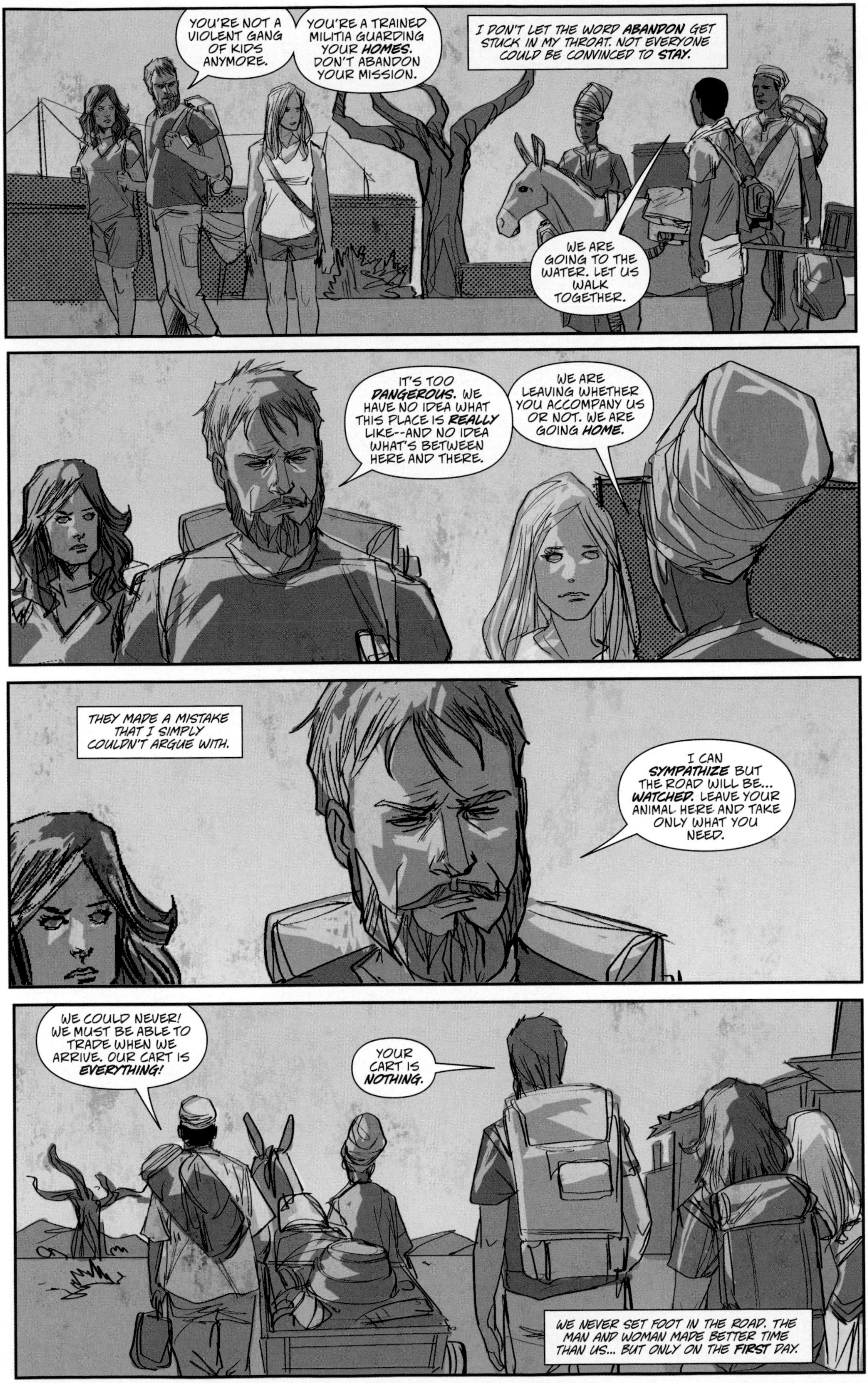
YOU'RE NOT A VIOLENT GANG OF KIDS ANYMORE.
YOU'RE A TRAINED MILITIA GUARDING YOUR **HOMES.** DON'T ABANDON YOUR MISSION.
I DON'T LET THE WORD **ABANDON** GET STUCK IN MY THROAT. NOT EVERYONE COULD BE CONVINCED TO **STAY.**
WE ARE GOING TO THE WATER. LET US WALK TOGETHER.
IT'S TOO **DANGEROUS.** WE HAVE NO IDEA WHAT THIS PLACE IS **REALLY** LIKE--AND NO IDEA WHAT'S BETWEEN HERE AND THERE.
WE ARE LEAVING WHETHER YOU ACCOMPANY US OR NOT. WE ARE GOING **HOME.**
THEY MADE A MISTAKE THAT I SIMPLY COULDN'T ARGUE WITH.
I CAN **SYMPATHIZE** BUT THE ROAD WILL BE... **WATCHED.** LEAVE YOUR ANIMAL HERE AND TAKE ONLY WHAT YOU NEED.
WE COULD NEVER! WE MUST BE ABLE TO TRADE WHEN WE ARRIVE. OUR CART IS **EVERYTHING!**
YOUR CART IS **NOTHING.**
WE NEVER SET FOOT IN THE ROAD. THE MAN AND WOMAN MADE BETTER TIME THAN US... BUT ONLY ON THE **FIRST** DAY.

I TRIED TO TELL THEM. IT WASN'T JUST NAIVE PILGRIMS THAT WERE LISTENING TO THE TRANSMISSIONS...WOLVES HEARD THEM TOO.
THEY DIED FOR A CART OF JUNK.
CAN'T YOU DO SOMETHING?
SURE, I COULD GET US KILLED. HOW ABOUT THAT?
A FEW OF THE LARGER GROUPS MADE IT BY THE ROAD GANGS, BUT THE SMALLER ONES NEVER STOOD A CHANCE.
I KNEW WHAT THEIR ANSWER WOULD BE--BUT I ASKED ANYWAY.
LAST CHANCE TO CHANGE YOUR MIND AND TURN BACK.

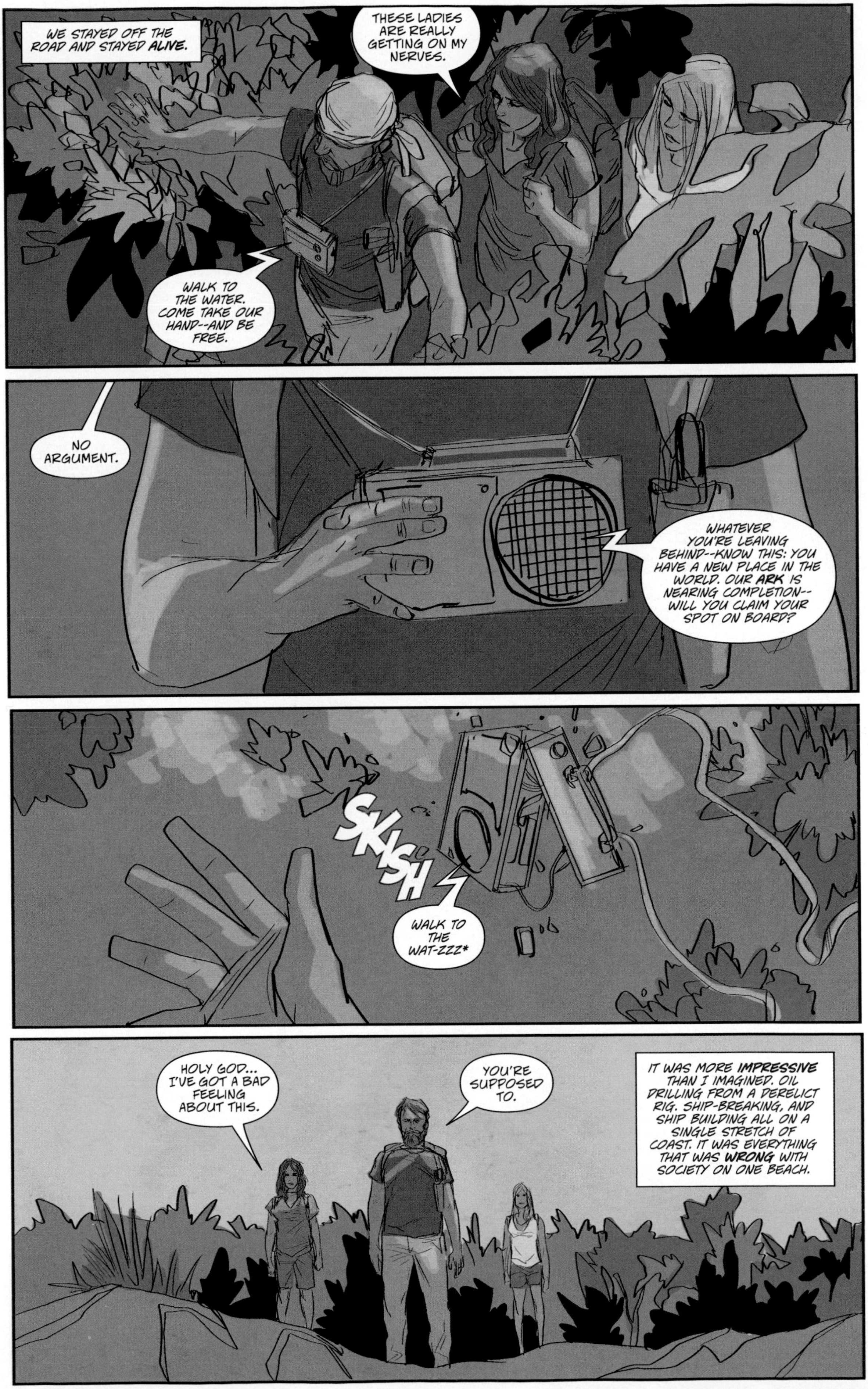
WE STAYED OFF THE ROAD AND STAYED **ALIVE**.
THESE LADIES ARE REALLY GETTING ON MY NERVES.
WALK TO THE WATER. COME TAKE OUR HAND--AND BE FREE.
NO ARGUMENT.
WHATEVER YOU'RE LEAVING BEHIND--KNOW THIS: YOU HAVE A NEW PLACE IN THE WORLD. OUR **ARK** IS NEARING COMPLETION--WILL YOU CLAIM YOUR SPOT ON BOARD?
SKISH
WALK TO THE WAT-ZZZ*
HOLY GOD... I'VE GOT A BAD FEELING ABOUT THIS.
YOU'RE SUPPOSED TO.
IT WAS MORE **IMPRESSIVE** THAN I IMAGINED. OIL DRILLING FROM A DERELICT RIG. SHIP-BREAKING, AND SHIP BUILDING ALL ON A SINGLE STRETCH OF COAST. IT WAS EVERYTHING THAT WAS **WRONG** WITH SOCIETY ON ONE BEACH.

THE GOAL IS TO GET ONTO THAT TANKER. IF WE BECOME SEPARATED YOU TWO MUST DO EVERYTHING YOU CAN TO STAY TOGETHER. AVOID THAT SLUM ON THE SAND AND GET ONTO THAT SHIP.
YOU CAN NEVER HAVE TOO MANY SURGEONS. IF I MAKE IT ON BOARD I'LL INSIST THAT SHE JOIN ME AS MY NURSE.

IF FORTUNATO WAS HERE, HE WOULD BE WORKING ON THE BEACH OR THE RIG. I COULD SMELL THE LEAKING OIL AND GAS FROM THE BLUFF.
I SAID GOODBYE TO THE WOMEN AND WE WALKED DOWN TO THE SAND.

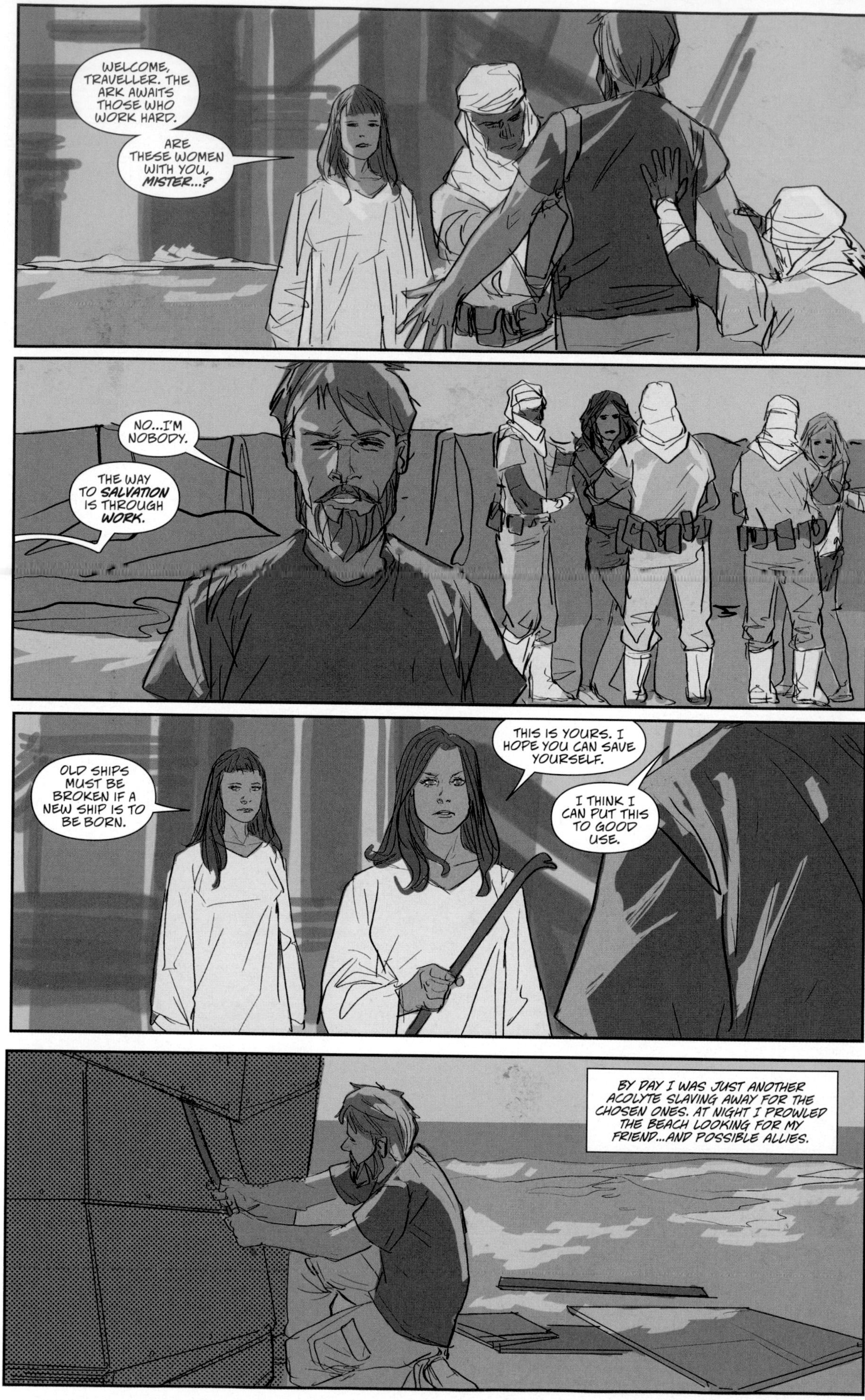
WELCOME, TRAVELLER. THE ARK AWAITS THOSE WHO WORK HARD.
ARE THESE WOMEN WITH YOU, MISTER...?
NO...I'M NOBODY.
THE WAY TO SALVATION IS THROUGH WORK.
OLD SHIPS MUST BE BROKEN IF A NEW SHIP IS TO BE BORN.
THIS IS YOURS. I HOPE YOU CAN SAVE YOURSELF.
I THINK I CAN PUT THIS TO GOOD USE.
BY DAY I WAS JUST ANOTHER ACOLYTE SLAVING AWAY FOR THE CHOSEN ONES. AT NIGHT I PROWLED THE BEACH LOOKING FOR MY FRIEND...AND POSSIBLE ALLIES.

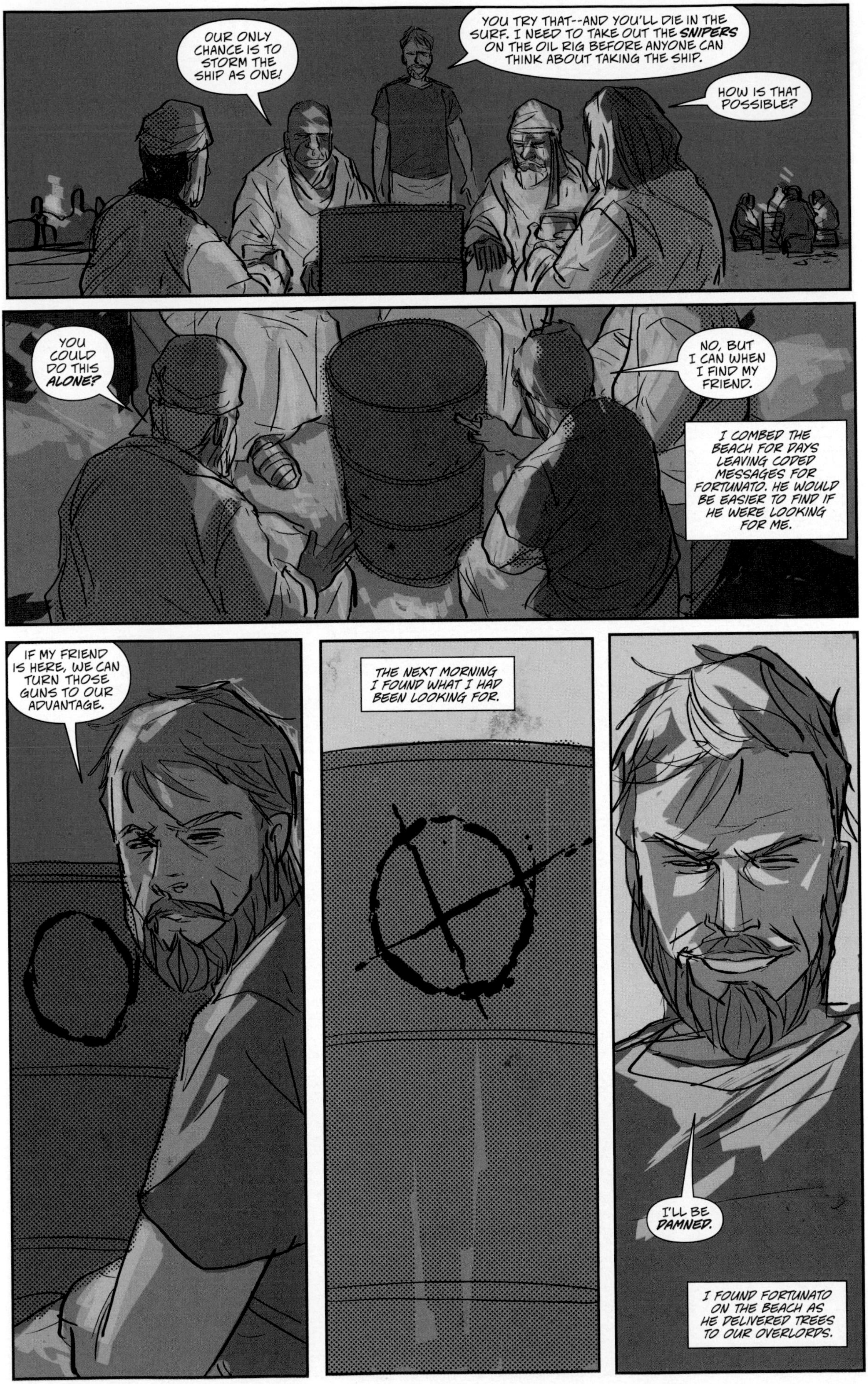
OUR ONLY CHANCE IS TO STORM THE SHIP AS ONE!
YOU TRY THAT--AND YOU'LL DIE IN THE SURF. I NEED TO TAKE OUT THE SNIPERS ON THE OIL RIG BEFORE ANYONE CAN THINK ABOUT TAKING THE SHIP.
HOW IS THAT POSSIBLE?
YOU COULD DO THIS ALONE?
NO, BUT I CAN WHEN I FIND MY FRIEND.
I COMBED THE BEACH FOR DAYS LEAVING CODED MESSAGES FOR FORTUNATO. HE WOULD BE EASIER TO FIND IF HE WERE LOOKING FOR ME.
IF MY FRIEND IS HERE, WE CAN TURN THOSE GUNS TO OUR ADVANTAGE.
THE NEXT MORNING I FOUND WHAT I HAD BEEN LOOKING FOR.
I'LL BE DAMNED.
I FOUND FORTUNATO ON THE BEACH AS HE DELIVERED TREES TO OUR OVERLORDS.

NEED A HAND?
YOU'RE LATE!
YOU WERE SUPPOSED TO HOBBLE RIGHT BEHIND ME!
I'M SORRY. BETTER LATE THAN NEVER? NOW...HOW MANY GUNS UP ON THE OIL RIG?
USUALLY ABOUT SIX. DO I EVEN WANT TO ASK WHY YOU'RE ASKING?
TO TAKE THIS TANKER YOU AND I ARE GOING TO ELIMINATE THOSE GUNS.
ONCE WE HAVE THE RIG, WE HAVE THE HIGH GROUND. THEN WE HELP TAKE THE SHIP.
EAT THIS AND GIVE ME THE SEEDS. I ENJOY WORKING WITH TREES. WHEN WE GET HOME I'M GOING TO BECOME A FARMER.
YOU'D BE A TERRIBLE FARMER.
I CAN LIVE WITH THAT.

OUR ORCHARD NEARS COMPLETION. BRING THIS NEW GIFT OVER HERE.
I'M GRATEFUL YOU'RE ALREADY ON BOARD. WHERE'S THE GIRL?
SHE'S WORKING DOWN IN THE GALLEY. THEY DIDN'T BUY THAT SHE'S MY NURSE. HOW ARE YOU? WE'VE BEEN WORRIED.
I'M FINE... BUT SOME ROUGH WEATHER'S MOVING IN TONIGHT.
YOUR JOB IS TO CARE FOR THE TREES--NOT TO DISTURB THE GARDEN.
I WONDER HOW ALL THESE TREES AND PLANTS WILL FAIR ON THE OPEN WATER IN THE SALT AIR? MANY OF THEM WILL NOT DO SO WELL, I THINK.
YOU ARE CAST OUT! NEVER RETURN TO THE ARK!
YOU'RE ALL DAMNED!
SO HOW ARE YOU GOING TO GET US ONTO THAT OIL RIG?
YOU'RE GOING TO HAVE TO DIE.
GREAT.

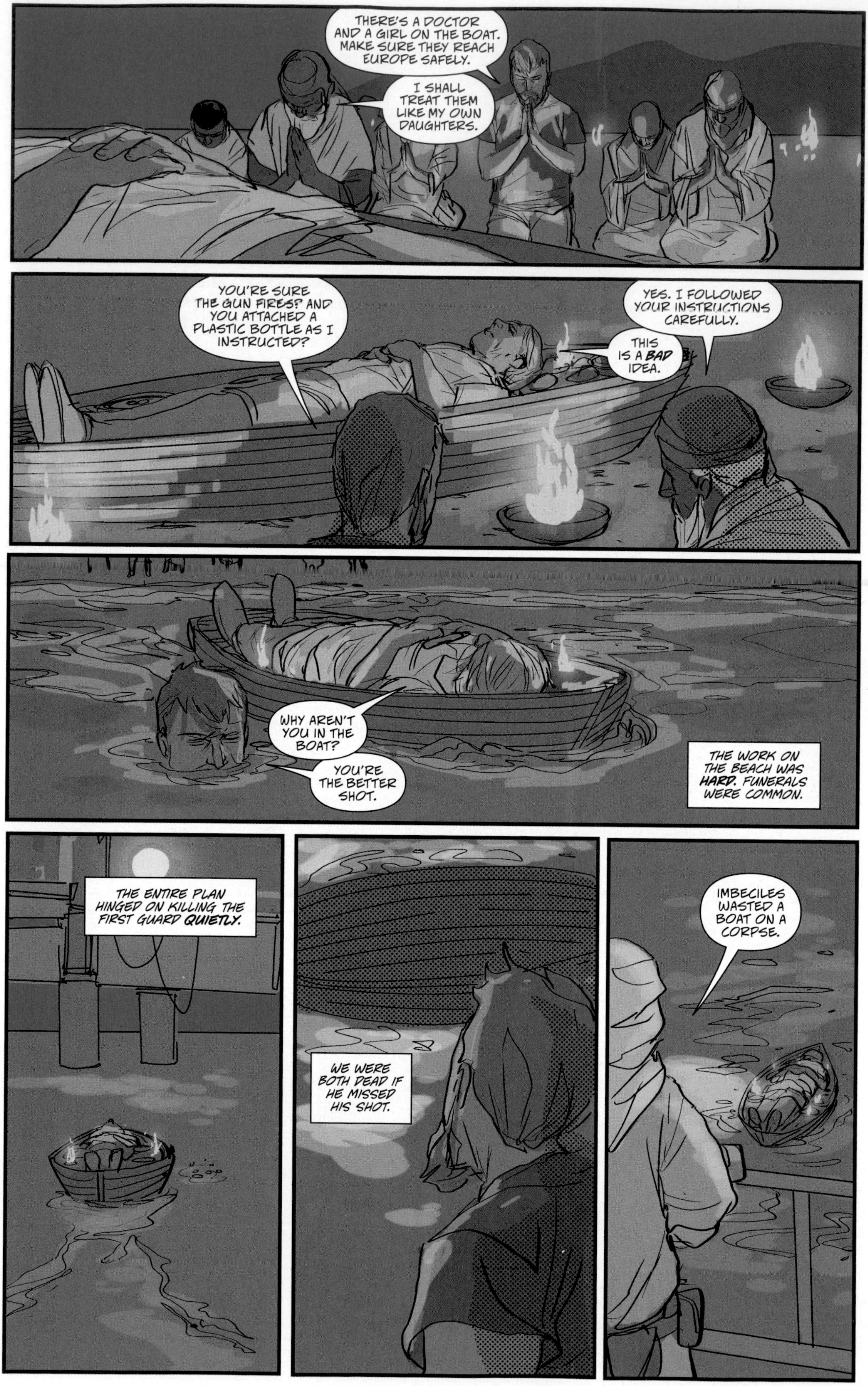

THERE'S A DOCTOR AND A GIRL ON THE BOAT. MAKE SURE THEY REACH EUROPE SAFELY.
I SHALL TREAT THEM LIKE MY OWN DAUGHTERS.
YOU'RE SURE THE GUN FIRES? AND YOU ATTACHED A PLASTIC BOTTLE AS I INSTRUCTED?
YES. I FOLLOWED YOUR INSTRUCTIONS CAREFULLY.
THIS IS A BAD IDEA.
WHY AREN'T YOU IN THE BOAT?
YOU'RE THE BETTER SHOT.
THE WORK ON THE BEACH WAS HARD. FUNERALS WERE COMMON.
THE ENTIRE PLAN HINGED ON KILLING THE FIRST GUARD QUIETLY.
WE WERE BOTH DEAD IF HE MISSED HIS SHOT.
IMBECILES WASTED A BOAT ON A CORPSE.

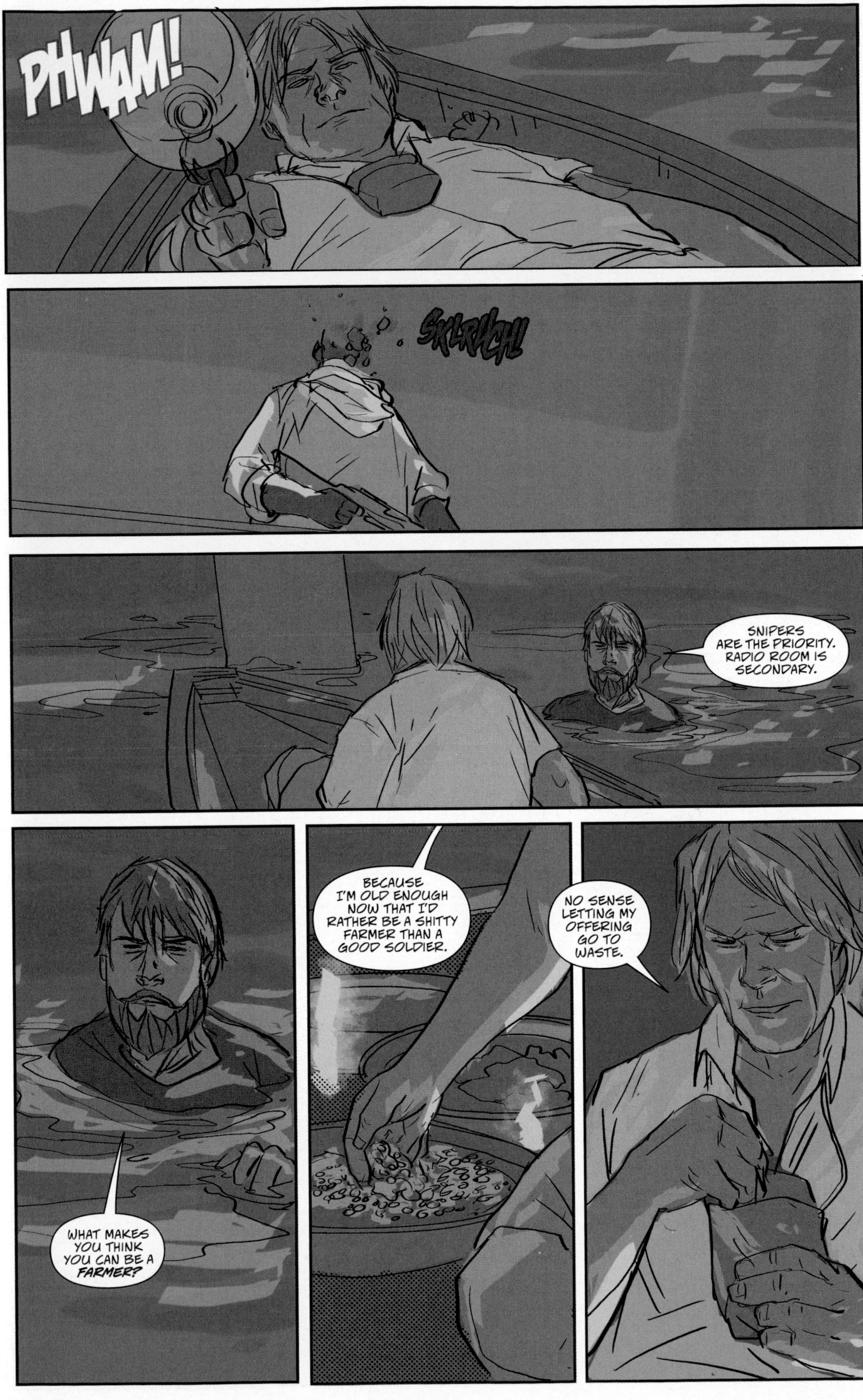
PHWAM!
SKLRUCH!
SNIPERS ARE THE PRIORITY. RADIO ROOM IS SECONDARY.
WHAT MAKES YOU THINK YOU CAN BE A *FARMER?*
BECAUSE I'M *OLD ENOUGH* NOW THAT I'D RATHER BE A SHITTY FARMER THAN A GOOD SOLDIER.
NO SENSE LETTING MY OFFERING GO TO WASTE.

THE WORKERS WERE CAGED BELOW DECK AT NIGHT, LEAVING ONLY THE GUARDS TOPSIDE. WE WORKED QUICKLY...
...AND QUIETLY.
YERK!
SHHK

TAKING THE RIG WAS THE EASY PART...
...AND WE DID IT WITHOUT FIRING A SHOT.
YAAAAAOOF!
KRUKCH
BEFORE IT GOT LOUD, WE SILENCED THE VOICES THAT WERE LURING PEOPLE TO THEIR DOOM.

IT'S TRUE THAT THIS FIRST ARK WILL SOON SAIL TO SALVATION BUT MORE VESSELS WILL BE PREPARED AND YOU CAN STILL FOLLOW US.
WHO ARE YOU? GET OUT OF--
THUNK KRAK!
IT'S ALL A LIE!
A DAMN LIE! THERE'S NO BOAT FOR YOU. THEY TAKE EVERYTHING YOU HAVE, AND WORK YOU TO DEATH! SPREAD THE WORD!
WE DON'T HAVE TIME FOR THIS. WE NEED TO TAKE THOSE SNIPERS NOW.
ARK TO RIG! A VERY UNFORTUNATE TRANSMISSION JUST WENT OUT FROM YOUR RADIO ROOM.
BWAM!
SPLUP

THAT'S A HIT. TWO TARGETS JUST--
I SEE THEM.
KABOOM
THEY'VE DONE IT! THE RIG IS OURS! EVERYONE GET TO THE TANKER! GO! GO!
WE HEARD FIGHTING ERUPT BELOW DECK...THE WORKERS THAT WERE CAGED IN AT NIGHT WERE FIGHTING THEIR WAY OUT. WE IGNORED IT AND DIRECTED OUR FIRE AT THE BOAT.
BAM
BAMBAM
BAM!
SPLACK
NO!
SKRESH
THE REMAINING GUARDS WERE OVERWHELMED...
...AND OUR ACT OF MERCY DOWN IN THE RADIO ROOM CAME BACK TO BITE US.
SHOT'S BLOCKED.
BEHIND--

YOU'VE DESTROYED EVERYTHING!
BLAM BLAM BLAM
NO!
UHN.
HE SHIELDED ME FROM HER WRATH.

GAKK
HKK. DAMN YOU...
I DON'T FEEL AN EXIT WOUND.
MY FAULT...
I SHOULD'VE KILLED HER...BUT I WAS JUST SO *TIRED* OF IT, YOU KNOW?
HANG ON, I'LL GET YOU TO THE TANKER AND WE'LL FIND THE DOC.
YOU NEVER REALLY PUT **ROOTS** DOWN. YOU NEED TO DO THAT.

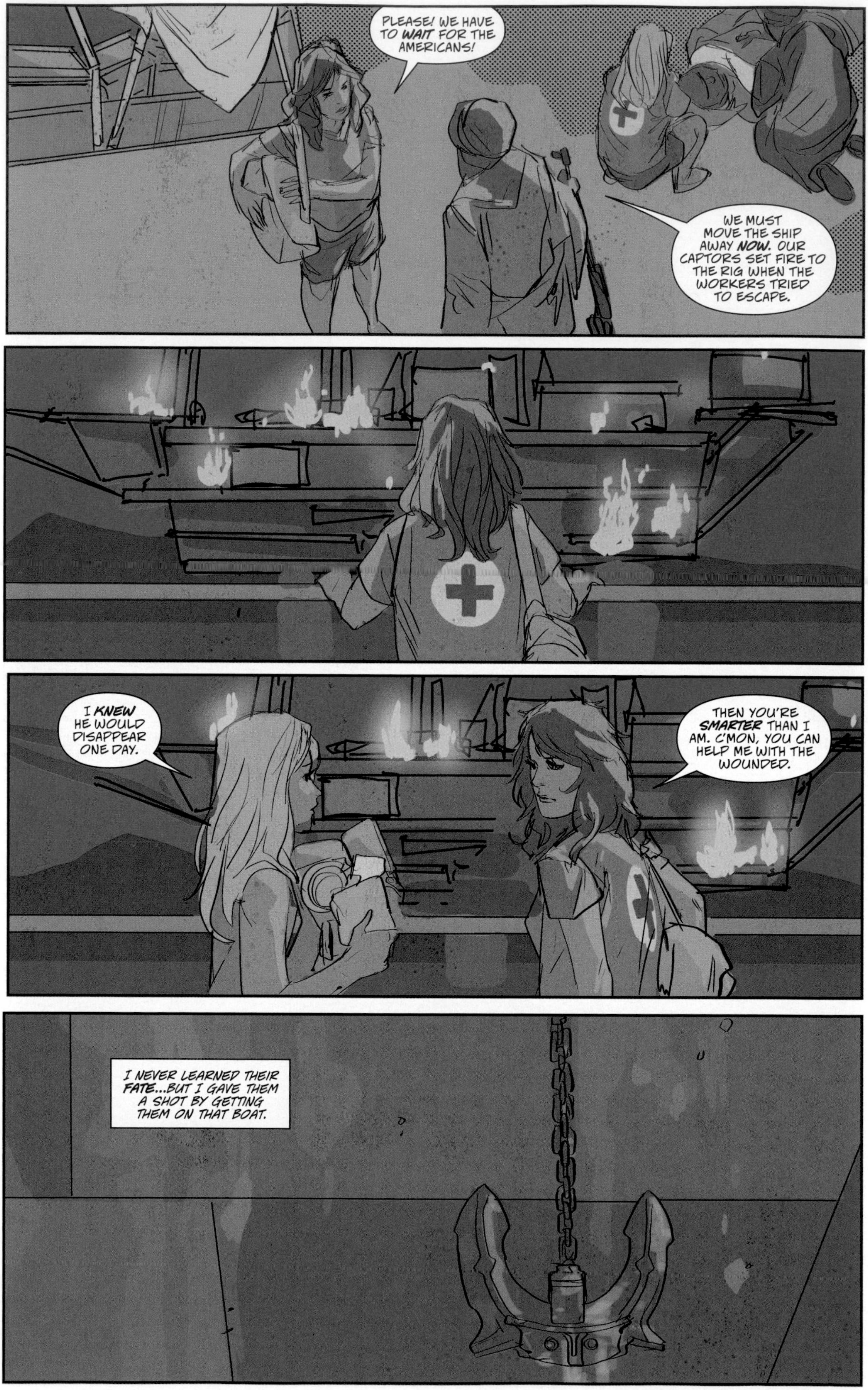
PLEASE! WE HAVE TO WAIT FOR THE AMERICANS!
WE MUST MOVE THE SHIP AWAY NOW. OUR CAPTORS SET FIRE TO THE RIG WHEN THE WORKERS TRIED TO ESCAPE.
I KNEW HE WOULD DISAPPEAR ONE DAY.
THEN YOU'RE SMARTER THAN I AM. C'MON, YOU CAN HELP ME WITH THE WOUNDED.
I NEVER LEARNED THEIR FATE...BUT I GAVE THEM A SHOT BY GETTING THEM ON THAT BOAT.

DON'T WORRY--THAT TANKER'S NOT THAT FAST.
YOU GOTTA MAKE IT BACK.
THANK YOU. FOR EVERYTHING.
THERE'S STILL A CHANCE--JUST HANG ON!
I PADDLED FURIOUSLY UNTIL MY FRIEND SLIPPED AWAY.

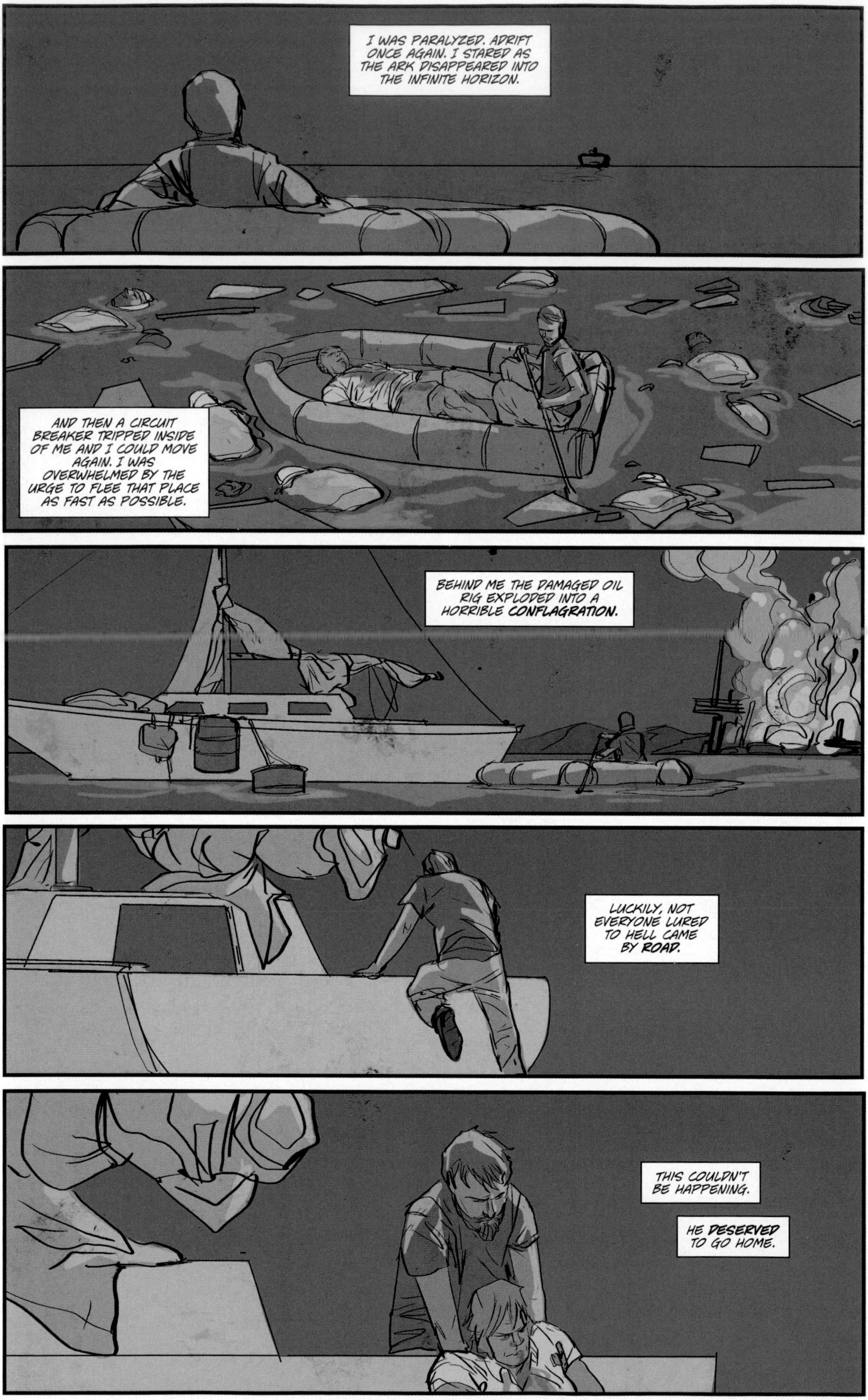
I WAS PARALYZED. ADRIFT ONCE AGAIN. I STARED AS THE ARK DISAPPEARED INTO THE INFINITE HORIZON.
AND THEN A CIRCUIT BREAKER TRIPPED INSIDE OF ME AND I COULD MOVE AGAIN. I WAS OVERWHELMED BY THE URGE TO FLEE THAT PLACE AS FAST AS POSSIBLE.
BEHIND ME THE DAMAGED OIL RIG EXPLODED INTO A HORRIBLE CONFLAGRATION.
LUCKILY, NOT EVERYONE LURED TO HELL CAME BY ROAD.
THIS COULDN'T BE HAPPENING.
HE DESERVED TO GO HOME.

THE SHAKES RIPPLED THROUGH MY HANDS AS THE ADRENALINE GAVE OUT
MY FRIEND HAD NO FAMILY OUTSIDE OF THE MEN AND WOMEN HE SERVED WITH.
I REACHED INSTINCTIVELY FOR HIS DOG TAGS. THEY WERE LONG GONE OF COURSE. LOST FOR MANY YEARS.
HE DIED WEARING SOMETHING SOFTER AROUND HIS NECK.

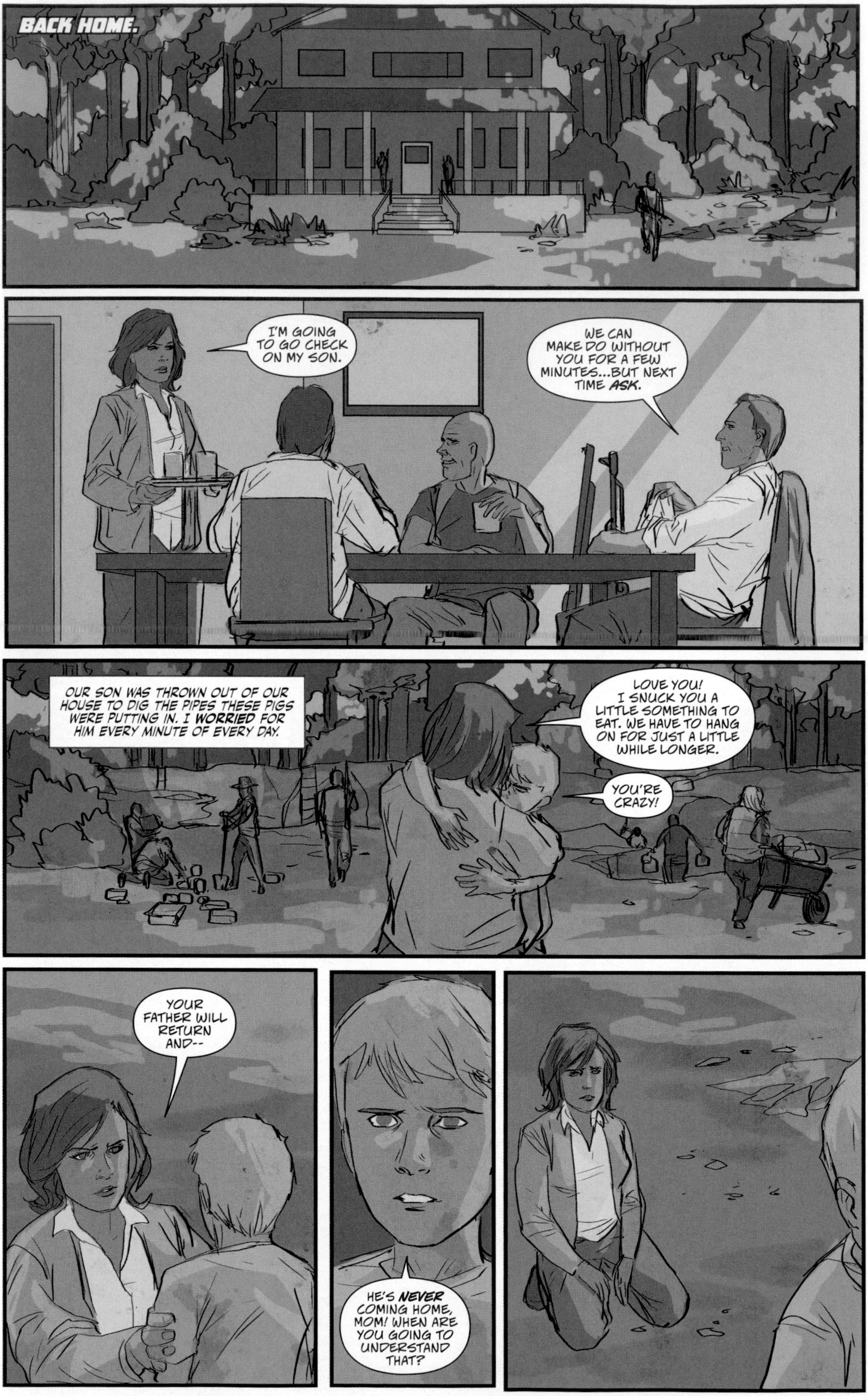
BACK HOME.
I'M GOING TO GO CHECK ON MY SON.
WE CAN MAKE DO WITHOUT YOU FOR A FEW MINUTES...BUT NEXT TIME ASK.
OUR SON WAS THROWN OUT OF OUR HOUSE TO DIG THE PIPES THESE PIGS WERE PUTTING IN. I WORRIED FOR HIM EVERY MINUTE OF EVERY DAY.
LOVE YOU! I SNUCK YOU A LITTLE SOMETHING TO EAT. WE HAVE TO HANG ON FOR JUST A LITTLE WHILE LONGER.
YOU'RE CRAZY!
YOUR FATHER WILL RETURN AND--
HE'S NEVER COMING HOME, MOM! WHEN ARE YOU GOING TO UNDERSTAND THAT?

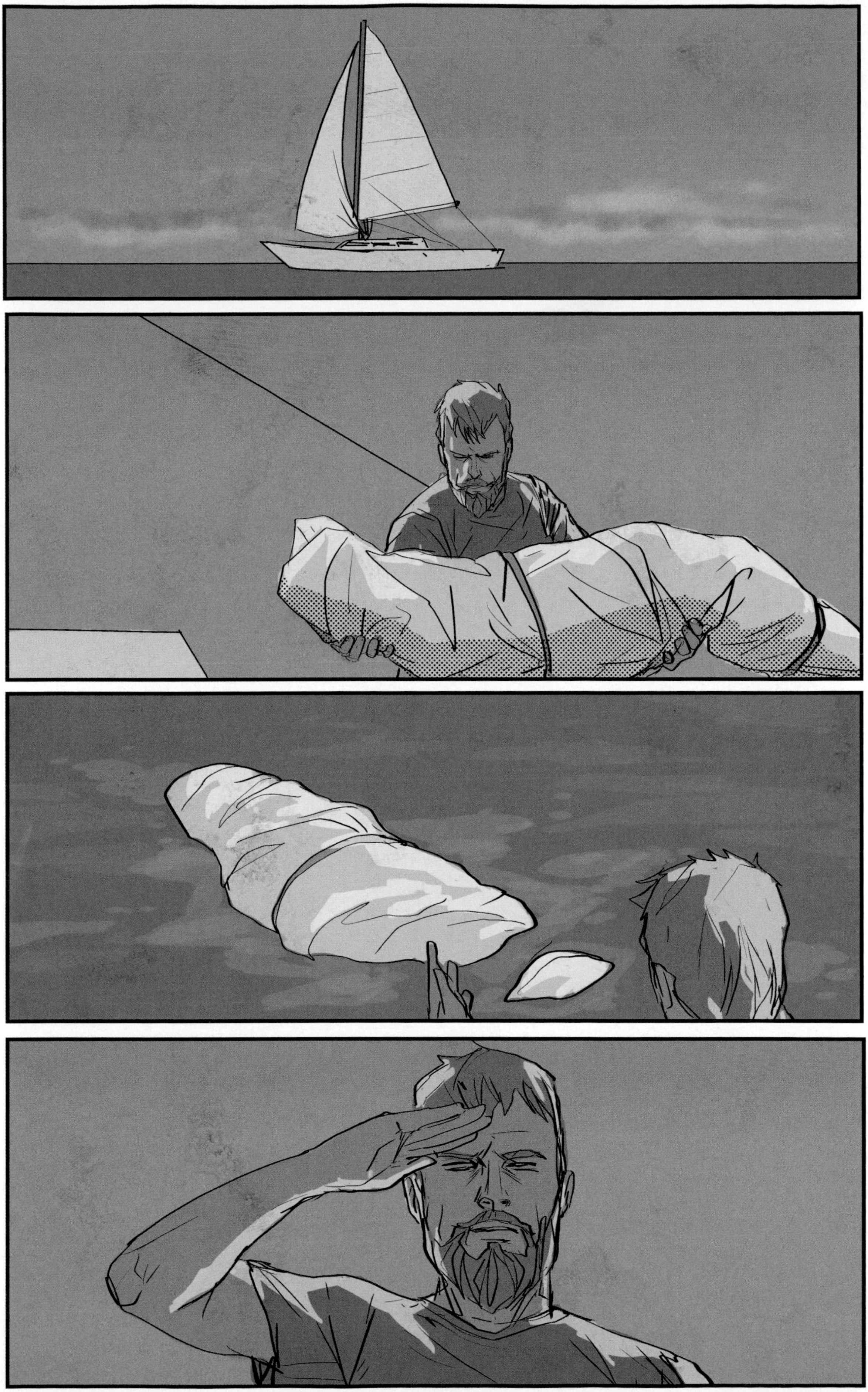

CHAPTER SIX
"Homecoming"

I SAILED CALM SEAS TOWARD A QUIET MANHATTAN. IT LOOKED DROWNED. DANGEROUS.
THE DREAD IN MY STOMACH FESTERED AS I NEARED LAND.
WERE MY WIFE AND SON SAFE? WERE THEY STILL ON OUR FARM? WERE THEY EVEN...
I SET THOSE THOUGHTS ASIDE.
I OPTED TO LAND IN NEW JERSEY.
I DIDN'T GET AS MUCH AS I WANTED FOR THE BOAT, BUT IT WAS ENOUGH TO BUY SOME GUNS. I DIDN'T WANT ANY WEAPONS, BUT I SUSPECTED I MIGHT NEED THEM.
ESPECIALLY IF MY WIFE AND SON WERE GONE.

FOR YEARS YOU RETURNED TO ME...IN DREAMS SO REAL THAT MY HEART WOULD SKIP A BEAT WHEN I WOKE UP ALONE.
MOM!
HE'S HERE!
MY HOPE FOR YOU IS NOW A BURDEN.
WHAT DID YOU SAY?
THE JUDGE IS RIDING UP THE ROAD RIGHT NOW. C'MON!
THE TRUTH IS, I CAN'T REMEMBER THE LAST TIME I DREAMT YOU WERE HOME.
OUR SON IS RIGHT...
OH.
...YOU'RE NEVER COMING BACK.

I WAS EXPECTING MORE THAN JUST ONE LAWMAN...HOW'S ONE MAN GOING TO BE ENOUGH TO GET RID OF THESE ANIMALS?
GET BACK UPSTAIRS.
THAT JUDGE IS EXPECTING TO MEET WITH THE OWNER OF THIS HOUSE TO FINALLY SETTLE A DISPUTE OVER SOME SQUATTERS.
HE *IS*.
ISN'T HE MEETING THE WOMAN THAT OWNS THIS DUMP RIGHT NOW?
THAT'S WHAT I HEARD.

LET ME GET THIS STRAIGHT: INSTEAD OF SERVING THESE MEN AN EVICTION NOTICE, YOU'RE SAYING YOU WANT THEM TO *STAY?*
WE'VE WORKED OUT A RENTAL AGREEMENT.
YOU WANT TO TALK IN *PRIVATE?*
THANK YOU, BUT NO. THAT'S NOT NECESSARY. WE'RE STARTING A FAMILY, TOO.
OH! WELL, GOOD FOR YOU. ONE LESS THING I GOTTA TAKE CARE OF. I'VE GOTTA CHECK OUT RUMORS OF A *BLOODBATH* DOWN THE WAY. TAKE CARE.
GO CAREFULLY, SIR!
GOOD LUCK TO YOU BOTH.

WE'RE HAVING A BABY? HOW ROMANTIC.
YOU WANTED HIM GONE, AND HE'S GONE. NOW WHERE'S MY MONEY?
NEVER TELL ANYONE ABOUT THIS, AND NEVER COME BACK.
EASIEST MONEY I EVER MADE.
WE GOTTA TALK. ANOTHER COUPLE OF GUYS HAVE DISAPPEARED.
DAMN IT. WHAT THE HELL IS GOING ON?
WHAT THE HELL ARE YOU LOOKING AT?
NOTHING.
GET YOUR HOMELESS ASS OFF MY FARM. THIS AIN'T A CHARITY OPERATION.
I SMOTHERED THE URGE TO BREAK HIS NECK RIGHT ON THE SPOT. I STUCK TO THE PLAN.
I HAD BEEN SURVEILLING MY HOME FOR DAYS, AND USING THE NIGHTS TO PICK OFF SOME OF THE TOUGHER CUSTOMERS.
I CAUGHT GLIMPSES OF MY WIFE THROUGH THE WINDOW. I WOULD FREE HER FROM CAPTIVITY OR DIE TRYING.

I HATE IT UP IN THE MOUNTAINS. THAT WOMAN BETTER START TO PLAY BALL SO WE CAN HEAD HOME.
SHE HAD HER CHANCE TO LEAVE. NOW THAT THE LAW'S OFF OUR DICK THAT BITCH IS ***DEAD.***
THAT NIGHT I HAD THAT SAME OLD DREAM AGAIN. YOU CAME BACK.
HEY, IS THAT ONE OF ***OUR*** GUYS?
HEY! STOP RIGHT THERE.
HELP...
THIS TIME WAS DIFFERENT. YOU SNUCK INTO OUR ROOM AND STOLE A KISS...AND PROMISED ME EVERYTHING WAS GOING TO BE FINE. THEN YOU WERE GONE AGAIN.
HE'S BACK! ***RUN!***
WHAT THE HELL?
WHO'S BACK?

AND WHEN I AWOKE YOUR BOW WAS MISSING.
THE OLD MAN IS BACK!
THWICK!
TWACK!
MUCH WAS TAKEN FROM US OVER THE YEARS. BUT NOTHING HAD GONE MISSING FROM MY BEDROOM...UNTIL THAT GLORIOUS MORNING.
GO TO HELL.
ALREADY BEEN.
MY HUSBAND WAS HOME.

I WENT INTO BATTLE FOR THE FIRST TIME WITHOUT **FEAR**. I WASN'T FIGHTING FOR MY COUNTRY, OR MY MEN. I WAS FIGHTING FOR MY **FAMILY**.
THEY COULDN'T SEE ME IN THE DARK AS THEY HUDDLED BY THEIR FIRES. COULDN'T HEAR MY BOW. THEY NEVER HAD A CHANCE.

I STARTED TO RECOGNIZE SOME FACES. THE GUY FROM THE ELECTRONICS STORE WAS GUARDING THE BARN.
THE BROTHERS THAT OWNED THE GAS STATION. BACK WHEN YOU COULD BUY GAS.
I NEVER LOST SLEEP FOR KILLING NEIGHBORS THAT SHOULD HAVE HELPED MY FAMILY.
BONG...BONG...BONG
LIKE BILL FROM DOWN THE ROAD...
BONG...BONG...
BEFORE MY LAST DEPLOYMENT I FED BILL'S CATTLE WHILE HE RECUPERATED FROM BACK SURGERY.
BONG...
BLAM!
THANKS FOR NOTHING, BILL.

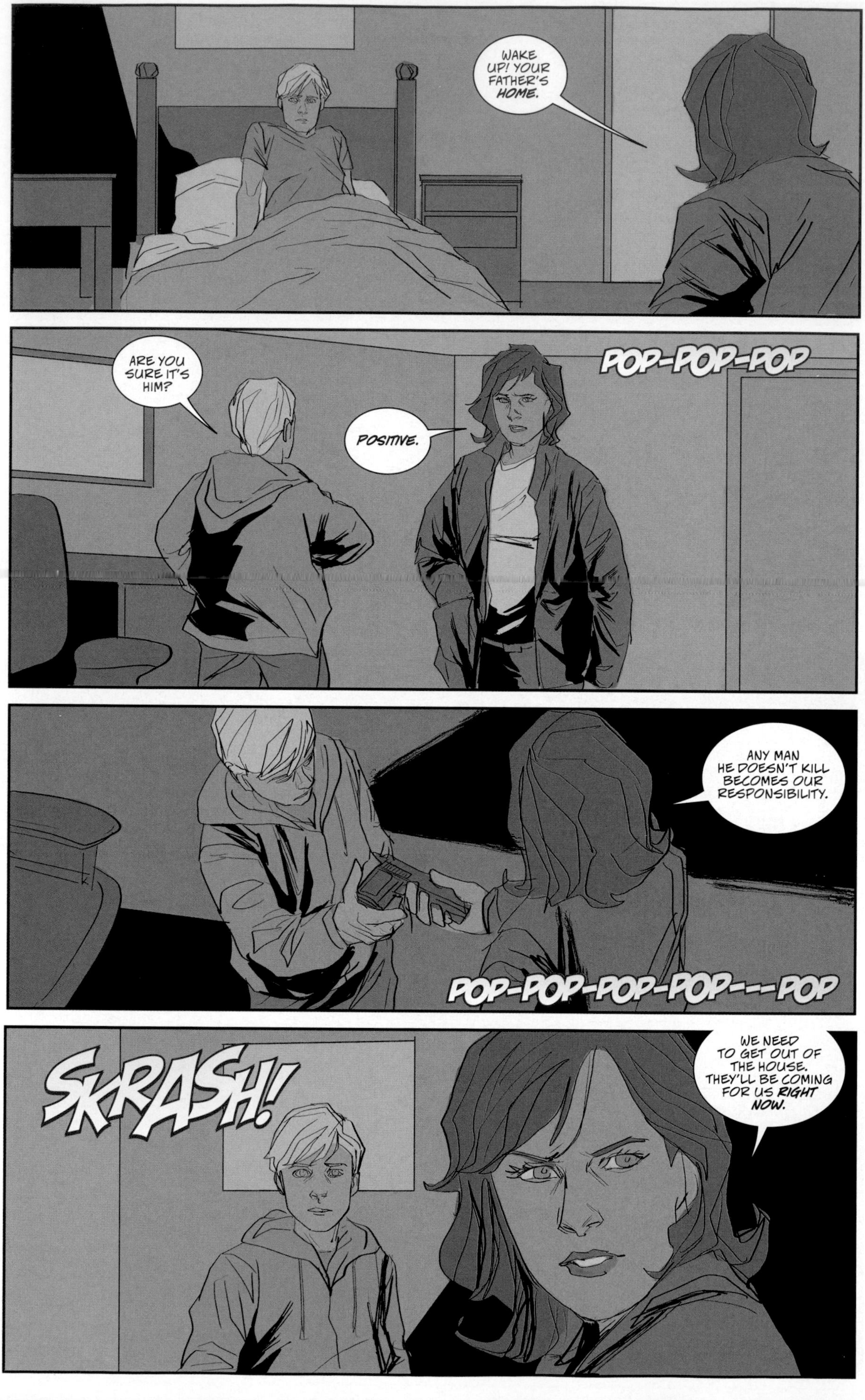
WAKE UP! YOUR FATHER'S *HOME.*
ARE YOU SURE IT'S HIM?
POSITIVE.
POP-POP-POP
ANY MAN HE DOESN'T KILL BECOMES OUR RESPONSIBILITY.
POP-POP-POP-POP---POP
SKRASH!
WE NEED TO GET OUT OF THE HOUSE. THEY'LL BE COMING FOR US *RIGHT NOW.*

I'LL GRAB THE WOMAN...
..YOU GRAB THE KID.
OH SHIT.
BLAM!
WAIT-
URK
BLAM!
GET OUT OF OUR HOUSE!
BLAM! BLAM! BLAM!

BOOM!
I HOLD MY BREATH AND LET MY LAST ARROW FLY AS I EXHALE. I TAKE MY TIME AND AIM MY SHOT.
THWUCK
UNLIKE THE AMATEUR IN THE BACK OF MY TRUCK.
ADIOS, ROBIN HOOD.
SKRISH
OH, CHRIST!
GUH

KRRABOOM!
MY GOD...ED'S STILL ALIVE UP THERE.
I MOMENTARILY LOST TRACK OF THE GUNMAN.
UNTIL I LOOKED UP.
SHHK
UHN. PLEASE...
...GIVE MY FRIEND UP THERE A BULLET.
DON'T HAVE THE BULLETS TO KILL A MAN TWICE.
DAMN YOU.

CLICK
BOOM!
I'M WALKING IN MY DOOR. ANYBODY THAT AIN'T MY FAMILY IS GETTING KILLED. ANY MAN THAT RUNS OUT THE BACK--I WON'T CHASE HIM DOWN.
FUCK YOU, ASSHOLE!
MAYBE WE SHOULDN'T ANTAGONIZE HIM.
BOOM!
SKREEEASH!
PENELOPE!
BOOM!

SPLACK!
WHERE'S MY FAMILY?
ALIVE. FOR NOW. GET IN HERE, KID.
YOU'RE ONE OF THE BUMS THAT'S BEEN LURKING AROUND.
THEY HAVE HER TIED UP.
SON.
WHERE'S YOUR MOTHER?
DROP THE GUN OR THEY BOTH DIE.
DAD, THERE'S A MAN--
I BROUGHT YOUR KNIFE HOME, TERRY.
IF I DIDN'T MAKE IT AT LEAST TERRY WOULD KNOW I STILL HAD MY BLADE...
...GIVE HIM A FIGHTING CHANCE.
WHUMP

THIS ISN'T HOW I IMAGINED OUR REUNION.
SORRY.
HOW MANY MEN ARE OUT THERE?
PRETTY SURE I KILLED THEM ALL.
DON'T PLAY GAMES WITH ME! HOW MANY MEN DO YOU HAVE, AND WHERE ARE THEY?
MY MEN ARE DEAD AND BURIED.
YOU EXPECT ME TO BELIEVE THAT YOU KILLED ALL MY MEN BY YOURSELF?
THE KILLING WAS EASY. HARD PART WAS DRAGGING THE BODIES BACK DOWN TO THE THRUWAY.

NOBODY HERE HAS TO DIE TODAY...EXCEPT THIS MAN. ANY MAN THAT WALKS AWAY NOW HAS MY WORD: I WON'T COME AFTER YOU.
I'M IN CONTROL HERE! NOT YOU!
LET ME TELL YOU SOMETHING...
I FOUGHT ON DAMN NEAR EVERY CONTINENT. ONE THING I LEARNED: YOU CAN WIN EVERY BATTLE, AND STILL LOSE A WAR. VICTORY NEEDS MORE THAN JUST BLOOD. IT REQUIRES YOU TO SNATCH YOUR ENEMY'S SPIRIT. YOU HAVE TO MAKE IT UNPOPULAR FOR HIM TO FIGHT.
THIS IS ALL SANCTIONED! IT'S NOT EVEN YOUR FARM ANYMORE!
I THINK I'LL LET THE MEN TAKE YOU BACK TO THE CITY ALIVE.
LET THE FAMILIES OF YOUR VICTIMS HAVE A GO AT YOU.
NOBODY'S COMING. YOU'RE LEFT BEHIND.

I DIDN'T ESCAPE HELL TO BE CHASED OFF MY OWN LAND BY THIEVES AND MURDERERS.
KILL YOU AND I WIN THE BATTLE, BUT WHEN EVERYONE CAN SEE WHAT IT COSTS TO FIGHT ME--**I WIN THE WAR.**

THAT UNSAVORY MESSAGE WAS SENT JUST A FEW MILES DOWN THE ROAD. I DON'T TAKE PLEASURE IN KILLING--EVEN THE MURDERERS AND ROAD AGENTS YOU CALL FRIENDS. AND I CERTAINLY DON'T ENJOY DECORATING A HIGHWAY WITH BODIES. BUT BARBARIANS ONLY UNDERSTAND A LANGUAGE OF VIOLENCE. I TOLD THEM NO.
YOUR REINFORCEMENTS GOT AN EYEFUL OF THAT GRISLY SCENE AND TURNED AROUND. THERE WASN'T EVEN A DISCUSSION.
THE IRONY IS, THOSE MEN WORK FOR ME NOW. THEY WENT HOME WITH THE STORY I WANT THEM TO TELL: STAY OUT OF THE CATSKILLS.

I DIDN'T SIGN UP FOR THIS.
ME NEITHER.
NOBODY'S LEAVING!
DIVIDE AND CONQUER.
KLUNK
GET AW--UHN.
HURRY, SON.
YEAAAAAANH
I KNEW WE HAD THE IDIOT WHEN HE DROPPED HIS GUN.

COVER THE GUN! TERRY, CUT ME FREE.
WHUDD
START RUNNING, BOY... STAY HERE AND YOU'RE GONNA SEE YOUR PARENTS DIE.
FINE. YOUR MOTHER GOES FIRST.
STOP IT!
SHUCK
OH GOD.
SORRY.

RAAAAAAARGH!
I DUG MY FINGERS INTO THE WOUND...
STOP! STOPGETOFF!
I CLAWED AND RIPPED UNTIL I HIT SOMETHING SLICK AND PULSING...
...AND GOUGED AWAY UNTIL THE SCREAMING STOPPED.

THERE'S SO MUCH I NEED TO TELL YOU. I DON'T KNOW WHERE TO BEGIN. SON, ARE YOU OK?
YES. I THINK SO. I DUNNO.
RELISH WHAT'S ABOUT TO HAPPEN, TERRY. BECAUSE YOUR FATHER IS ABOUT TO SAY SOMETHING HE RARELY DOES.
SORRY I'M *LATE*.

OVER TIME I TOLD THEM MY STORY. ALL OF IT. WELL, ALMOST ALL OF IT.
WE TENDED OUR FARM AND KEPT TO OURSELVES.
SHARED WITH NEIGHBORS WHEN WE COULD. STEERED CLEAR OF THE **TROUBLES**.
WE FOUND WAYS TO REMEMBER OUR **FRIENDS**.
JOE
FAMILY.
IT WAS TIME TO BURY THE PAST.
MY FIGHT WAS OVER.

BUT I KNEW BETTER. I HAD SOMETHING WORTH TAKING.
A HOME. A FAMILY. **LOVE.**
I HAD TO BE PREPARED FOR AGGRESSION.
LIVING IN PEACE CARRIED ITS OWN **BURDEN** FOR ME. THAT WAS A QUIETER BATTLE THAT WE WON AFTER A FEW SEASONS.
WE HAD ALL THE TIME IN THE WORLD. I WASN'T GOING ANYWHERE.
JOE

I WAS HOME.
JOE
THE END

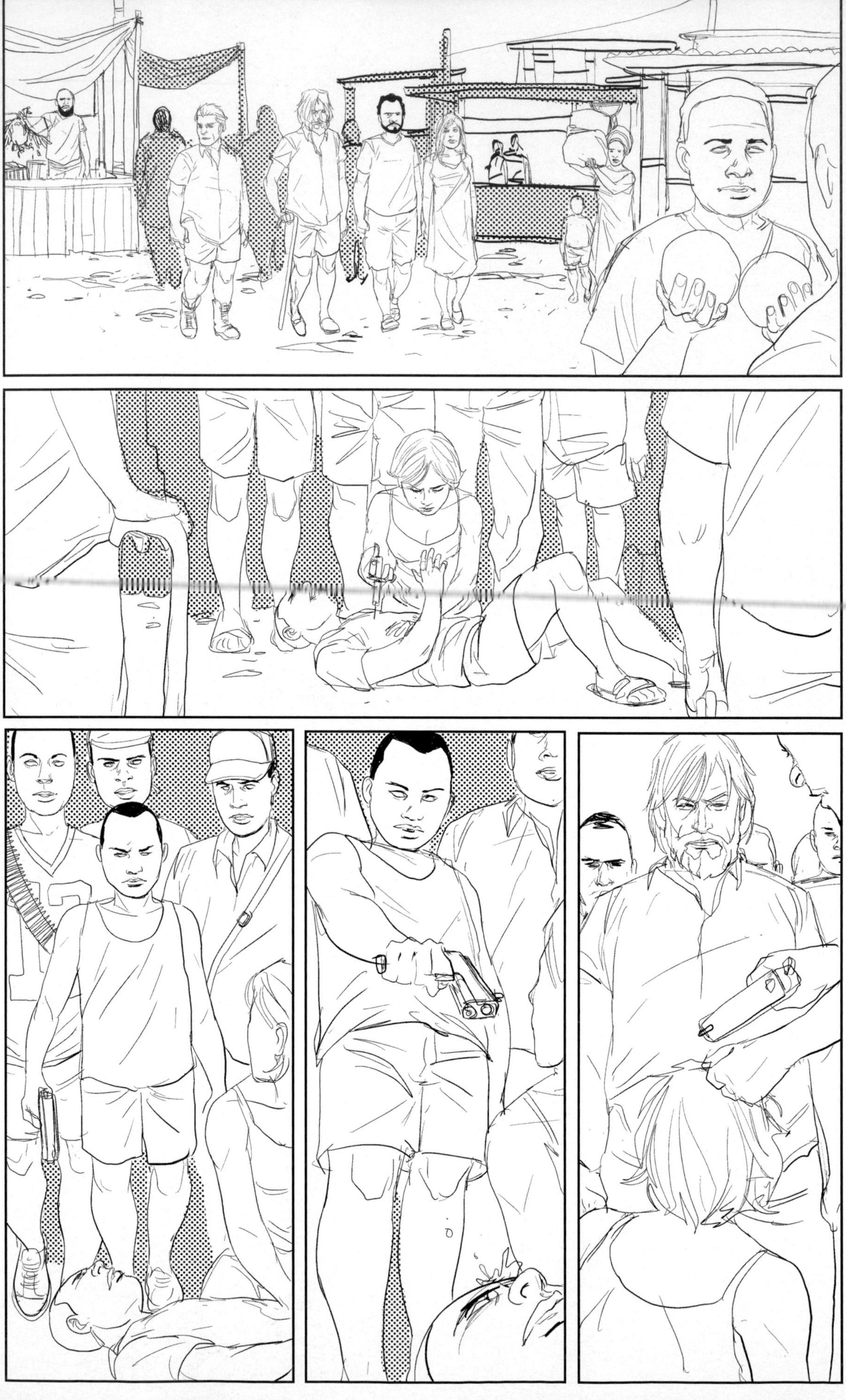

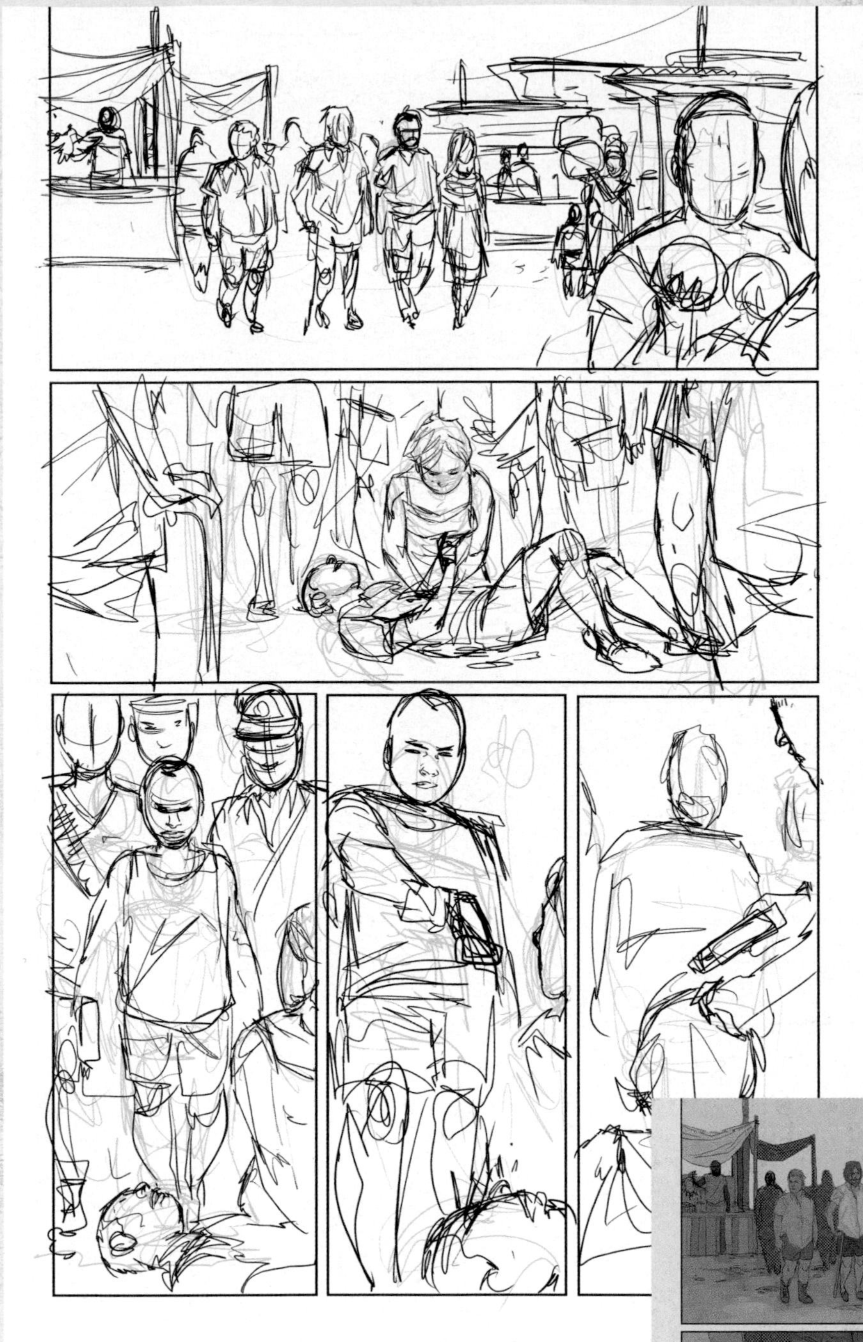

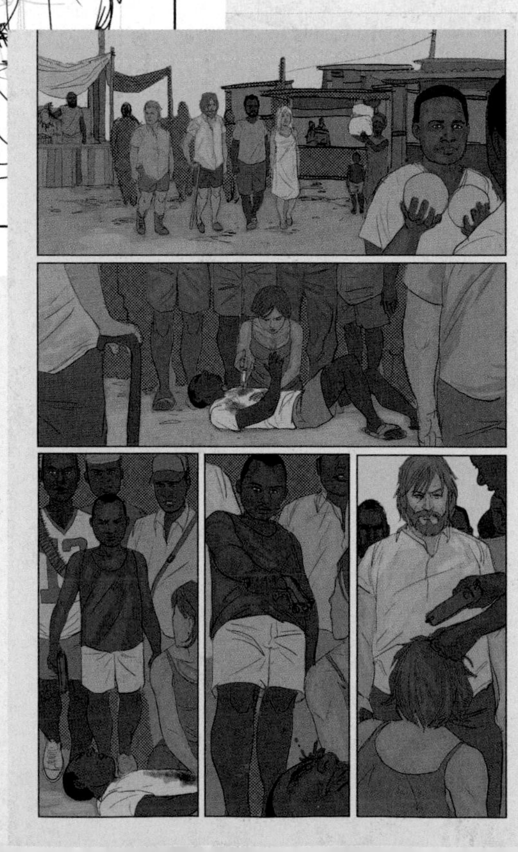

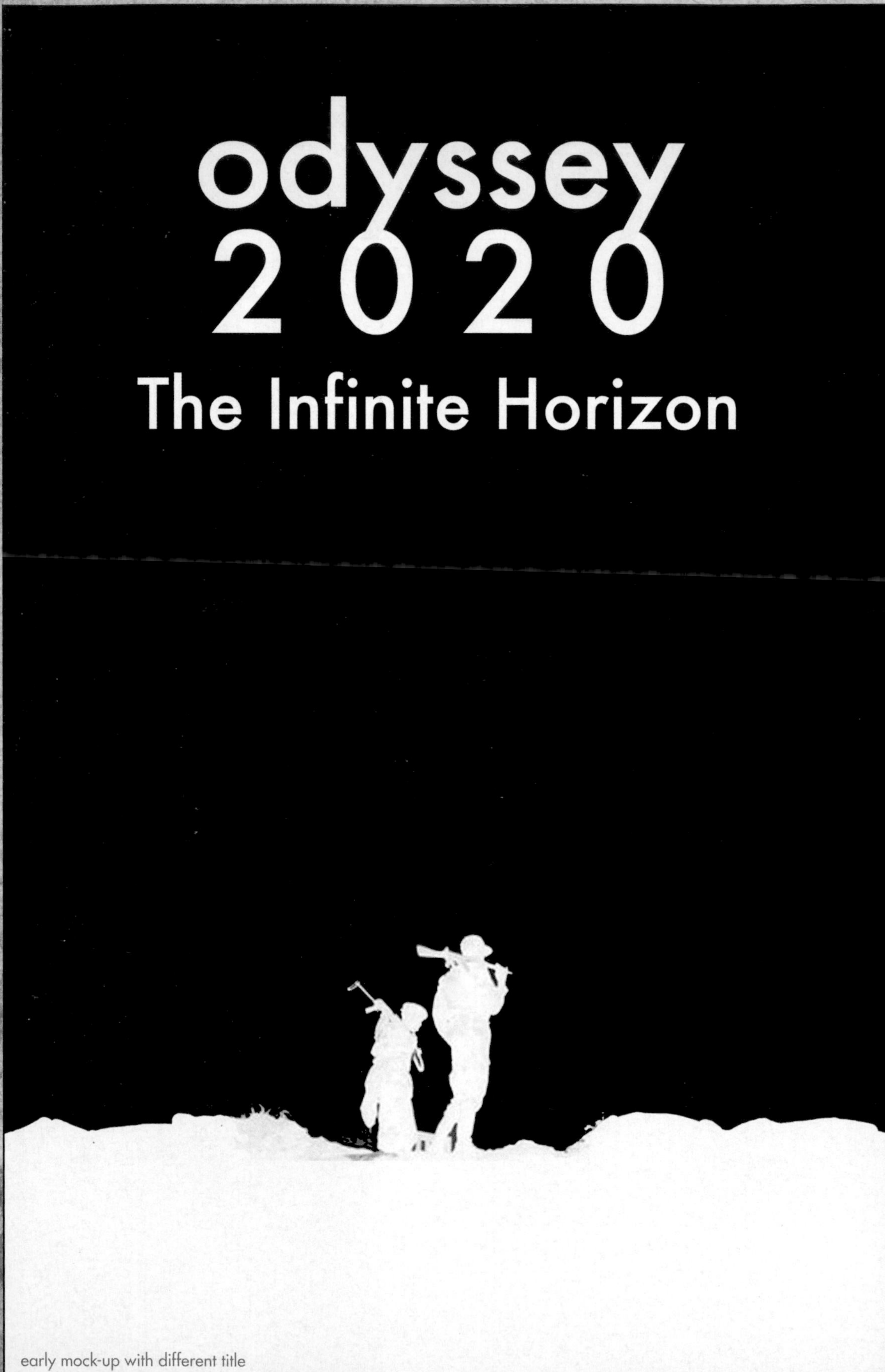

early mock-up with different title